SB
455   Hersey, Jean, 1902–
.H494 Gardening and being

Gardening and Being

Also by Jean Hersey

The Touch of the Earth
A Widow's Pilgrimage
Change in the Wind (with Robert Hersey)
These Rich Years (with Robert Hersey)
The Shape of A Year
A Sense of Seasons
Carefree Gardening
Woman's Day of Houseplants
Garden in Your Window '~
Halfway to Heaven

❀ *Jean Hersey*

GARDENING AND BEING

Continuum · *New York*

Grateful acknowledgment is made to Hill and Wang, a division of Farrar, Straus and Giroux, Inc. for permission to reprint the poem "No More, No More" from *That Shining Place* by Mark Van Doren, copyright © 1969 by Mark Van Doren; and to Alfred A. Knopf, Inc. for permission to reprint lines from *The Prophet* by Kahlil Gibran, copyright © 1923 by Kahlil Gibran and renewed 1951 by administrators C.T.A. of Kahlil Gibran Estate, and Mary G. Gibran.

1982

The Continuum Publishing Company
575 Lexington Avenue
New York, N.Y. 10022

Library of Congress Cataloging in Publication Data

Hersey, Jean, 1902-   Gardening and being.

1. Gardening. 2. Gardening–Pennsylvania. I. Title.
SB455.H494   635'.01   81-17309
ISBN 0-8264-0188-0   AACR2

For Jane

Contents

1. *October Is Change* 1

2. *November Is Appreciating* 14

3. *December Is Giving* 26

4. *January Is Holding* 37

5. *February Is Not to Hurry* 49

6. *March Is to Be Aware* 60

7. *April Is Living This Moment* 72

8. *May Is Listening* 85

9. *June Is to Loose and Let Go* 97

10. *July Is Accepting* 108

11. *August Is Blessings* 119

12. *September Is Confidence* 131

Help us to be always hopeful
Gardeners of the Spirit
Who know that without darkness
Nothing comes to birth
As without light nothing flowers
                Author Unknown

Foreword

This is a book about gardening and being. It covers a full year, from October through September. Some months are more about gardening than being, and some are more about being than gardening, and some are an even mix.

I am inviting you to travel with me through this year in time— this year of gardening and being.

1 ❀

October Is Change

Take a winter wind, a summer sun, and mingle the two; add a wash of brilliant colors, and you have October. Some days will be still and sunny as Indian summer comes along; others will be crisp and cool. Through the month the colors spread gradually until the whole world around us is flamboyant and gay. We enjoy the pageant from the beginning to the peak later in the month.

Crosslands, the retirement center in Pennsylvania where I live, is in the country surrounded by fields and woodland and a few farms here and there. It is an ideal place from which to appreciate autumn, and other seasons too. On the 125 acres there are buildings to house over four hundred people, single men and women and couples. I live on the ground floor of a two-story building. We all have terraces and little gardens around them. I and others located along the south side of this building have a superb view of a valley with a charming hillside across from it and a brook at the bottom.

The sun pours into my apartment all day. In the evening I can see the moon come up, and if I am up in time, I can see the sun rise in the morning. Usually I am not.

When I came to Crosslands I made a few resolutions; the first one was that I would no longer hurry. Like most people, I have gone through stages when I have been frantically busy—when my children were little and growing and my husband was working. As you reach the retirement years, things slow down if you let them. Many people prefer to be as busy in retirement as before. More power to them. I, however, do not. I want, in these years, to have more time to be and less need to do. By no means am I a recluse. I love people and parties and travel. I indulge in all three, going to and giving parties and making visits to friends and family in faraway places. My two sons, Bob and Tim, and their families live in California, and I love going out to see them. My daughter, Joan, lives in Boston, and we visit back and forth.

Also, I like to sew, to read, to hook rugs, to walk, and to swim (there is an indoor pool here where a number of us swim nearly every day). Above all, I like to garden. I moved here two years after my husband died and have been here three years now. I like it very much.

Beginnings are so interesting, so filled with promises and possibilities. Almost all kinds of beginnings—the beginning of a year, a month, a day. Especially a month. What will it bring? What will it take away—this month of October? We are always gaining something, and losing something else as we go through the different intervals of our lives. We are always moving forward or backward, for we never stand still. Moving backward can be a part of our growth, too, but we may not see it at the time. We may feel quite out of sorts and discouraged as we slip. But the next week or month we are aware that we learned something from our backward movement. Our forward-moving moments, when we sense growth, are the most thrilling. Often, at the time, we know that something is occurring. We may not think much about growth, but it is there.

Two months ago I put two glasses of water with wax paper fastened over the top with elastic bands on the dresser in my bedroom. I put five holes in the paper in each glass and arranged ten African violet leaf stems, two from each of my plants, through the holes and into the water. Now, on these ten leaves, new rootlets have formed. Here is another beginning I am excited about. It is more than a mere ten leaves in water. It is the beginning of new life. I hold them over the lamp every night and look at them while a little prickle wanders up my spine at this new beginning I am watching and participating in.

This is the month when indoor gardens come to the fore. In the living room I have five African violet plants, each one different—two shamrocks and two trailing philodendrons and a sea onion. This is my total indoor garden. It is just the right size for my apartment.

This morning I spread newspapers on the grass beyond my terrace and took out my African violet plants, the rooting leaves, and a pail full of luscious, rich earth from the vegetable garden stirred up with some potting soil and mushroom soil. These violets have bloomed for five years with barely a pause. Now they need replacing and, until then, repotting. So I repotted them, grooming off old leaves. Having had them so long, each one is an old friend. I shall regret parting with them, but that is why I am rooting new leaves. These I also put in small pots. Their roots are full of promise. I know it will be a long time before new leaves appear above the surface of their earth, but I shall be watching and waiting.

I feel that each month has a message for us. What is the message of October? This is the month of change. For me, this year, the message of October is to learn to flow with the changes that come into my life, changes in all areas of living and being. Nature's most drastic change this month is from lush green foliage to bare trees and vines. Can we accept the changes in our lives as gracefully and beautifully as the landscape does in autumn?

Change isn't always easy to take, yet life means change. So we have to learn. When we are younger we can better manage alterations in our living patterns. But as we get older it becomes more difficult to accept some of the different things that occur. Yet it is important for us not to buck the new events, but to adjust and adapt to them, to incorporate them into our lives with grace.

There are no rules for adapting to change. Each of us must find his or her own way. But possibly there are a few guidelines. Can we consider each of the changes in our lives, our days, our circumstances, as a new era, a new beginning, a learning and growing experience? If we can, then change is easier to accept. Of course, some of the different circumstances that come to us are welcome ones. We can coast along with these, with no problem. If we can embrace all kinds of changes and follow where they lead, we free ourselves from tension, and our lives become richer and more worthwhile. This seems to me the message of October—to learn to accept the challenge of change.

I like to go out and view my little terrace garden often. It is so small and charming. The gardens I have had before now have been much larger—right for their time as this one is right for me now. You reach my small garden through double glass doors from the living room. When I moved here I had Mr. Manni, of Lenape Nursery, come and do a landscape design and plant the garden. It consists mostly of dwarf evergreens. The main feature is a small weeping birch. The design and arrangement are lovely all year. I have a few perennials and, in summer, I add annuals for color and gaiety.

Now, during this season, the dwarf marigolds are a blazing gold, the ageratum a deep blue. The heliotrope waves its laden branches in all directions, and the zinnias add to the garden with their brick-red and yellow flowers.

In early September I bought eight chrysanthemum plants in a variety of colors, and I have loved watching them come out. I have yellow, copper, white, and lavender ones. They are magnificent right now. This morning I was in the garden to pick a few marigolds for a miniature bouquet. They were dazzling in the morning sun. There was a snail on a blossom. Usually I squash snails, but this one was so young, so vulnerable and appealing with his tiny, curled-up shell and delicate feelers. Why should I deprive him of enjoying this Indian summer day? I left him eating a marigold petal and gathered my flowers beyond him.

I looked at all the blossoms around me with a glow of pleasure and pride. They were at their peak. And then I realized that the wonder and glory of a garden resides in more than meets the eye. There are the roots burrowing deeply down, seeking nourishment. There is the Life Force undergirding and filling all that grows here in this small area. This Life Force reaches out from all my flowers, yes, and the little snail, too, to the green grass beyond, to the neighbors' gardens, and to the valley and hillside of trees farther away.

All at once, in the valley, I see an early indication of autumn, the first tree to turn a coppery tone; there it stands among its green neighbors, an individualist. The sun picks it out, and it positively glows. There is something stirring about the first hints of a new season.

Last night, at Fran's apartment, I experienced my first grate fire of the fall. How beautiful is a blazing hearth on a cool evening. There is magic in the flames curling around the wood and the shower of sparks that burst out when a new log is put on.

Fran and I had dinner in her apartment, and afterward we spent a stimulating evening talking. One of the best of all beginnings is the start of a new friendship. As you feel a little more trust in your new friend each time you meet, you let out a little more of yourself, and your friend does too. You find a little more to share. In the three years I have been at Crosslands, I had never met Fran until just recently. I sense something pleasant and new springing into being between us.

The leaves are falling off my weeping birch tree, perhaps because of the drought. Whenever one drops, there remains a slim, pointed, dark green, firm bud, which will come out next spring.

Isn't there always a hint of what will be in what is?

This morning I woke to a peak experience. My valley was filled with heavy white mist thinning toward the top. The sky above the trees across the valley was gold. What a moving moment. Here and there a tree shape stood out of the mist. I say "my valley" because I feel that if you love something, or some place, deeply enough, it becomes, in a sense, yours. I love this valley in all its moods and seasons.

The mist is now shifting, gradually disappearing toward the top of the valley. The gold sky above pales to ivory, but where the sun will soon rise it is deep orange. The heavy mist still lying in the bottom of the valley thins while I watch and rises in a broad band, gradually turning an orange-gold so brilliant I can scarcely look at it. My little weeping birch stands silhouetted against this gold mist. Now, the sun rises above the treetops. Shafts of sunlight filtering through the mist catch and highlight a few trees. The sun, fully up, streaming on the grass, turns it golden green. Here and there the dew sparkles among the blades.

All at once, another Indian summer day is born.

I must eat breakfast and take the car to the garage for a little servicing. Life is like that, an interesting mix of the ordinary and the peak experience. As long as we do what needs doing and keep the awareness of the mystery that permeates our daily happenings, there will be a lovely rhythm in our lives.

What a brilliant morning this was, with the sun shining all across the living-room floor as it does this time of year. My African violets seem to sparkle in the window, and the shamrock with the sun on it is a shimmering bright green. This is the kind of day when anything can happen, and all of it good, a day when, without thinking, you find yourself breathing deeply and standing tall, a morning when you are glad to be alive. A hint of winter moves through the air, mingled with the warmth of Indian summer—a typical October day.

This is the month we change our closets: bring winter clothes out, put summer ones away. We greet last year's woolens with delight—colors and textures we haven't worn for a long time. We put away all the lightweight cottons and silks and gay, summer colors. This is the time when indoors is very prominent in our lives. It is pleasant to sit in the living room and sew or read or have a friend over for tea and toast. It is also the month to wrap yourself in a blanket and sit outdoors on the terrace.

One of the delightful aspects of gardening, indoors or out, is that you are always dealing in the now and the future, seldom the past. Gardening is a forward-moving pastime. True, you might have a fleeting memory of the fragrance and beauty of last year's lilacs; but linked with this thought is that next year there will be even more flowers on the bush. And can there be a fragrance more appealing? The chrysanthemums, now in their full glory of bloom, are more exciting than even last spring's daffodils, sensational as they were at the time. As I look at my newly potted African violet leaves, I envision their first flowers, which will come a year from now.

I am looking out my glass doors beyond the terrace at the trees on the hillside across the valley. Last week there was but one, coppery-tinted, standing in the morning mist. Today there are several; also some red and yellow trees. Next week there will be more. Everywhere, every day now, leaves are turning. The oak tree near the Center is a coppery red.

There is so much sky here. I just came back from a walk, and it made me feel good—so expansive and inspired—to look up, over, and around, and see blue sky everywhere. The sky was covered with large sweeps of mackerel clouds. They always used to mean rain, but not these last few months since we have had our drought. Mackerel skies come and go, and no rain accompanies them.

One reason there is such a vast and spacious feeling here is that, where our buildings are, used to be wide-open corn fields. I like to think that, where my terrace stands, the land was once plowed in great furrows and planted with corn, and later on, right where I sit, were clusters of waving, golden corn tassels. It lends such a pleasant note to my musings when I settle on the terrace with my sewing or a book.

On my walk this morning I passed the lovely planting that Holly had done in memory of her husband. Some of the bushes are turning red and bronze. There was a row of scarlet euonymus. I stopped and picked off a handful of brilliant leaves. Farther on, I gathered gold leaves. Every October I send my son Bob and his wife, Susan, in California a handful of fall leaves, lest they forget the beauty of autumn colors in the East.

There is a circular route you can walk here, on the road through the property of Crosslands around a sort of casual horseshoe shape. Joining the sides of the shoe is a path by the pond. This makes a one-mile walk, and I do it each day. It is pleasant in every season. Now you see everyone's little terrace garden full of gold and purple and bronze chrysanthemums, and on the pond as you pass there are always a few ducks. They amuse you with their divings and landings on the water, creating large and small V's of ripples behind them.

For no known reason I was feeling a little low-spirited when I set out today. But one look at the sky and the magnificent vastness of it filled my being and lifted my spirits. Gathering colored leaves set me on high, and I returned home in quite a different mood.

Elizabeth Vining is coming for lunch. When I returned from my walk, I set the table, made the salad with my tomatoes, cut up the mushrooms. We are having creamed mushrooms on toast, salad, and raspberries from the garden. How I love eating garden produce!

Sometimes I think there are five seasons—winter, spring, summer, fall, and Indian summer. We are deep in Indian summer now. A few days ago it was cold as winter. We were all wearing heavy coats. A wild wind blew, reminding me that I am not very fond of cold winds, or winter either. But today it is summer again, no, Indian summer. These days have a special quality. They are neither summer nor fall. There is a smoky blueness in the air in the morning and at dusk. If you walk around, you don't need a sweater, but if you sit there is a chill around the edges, and you want a wrap. Across the valley the hillside of trees is becoming more and more colorful, and the shadows between the trees are very blue. People are out watering their gardens. The earth is so dry.

The air is still. Now and then a great flock of blackbirds gathers in the valley trees and presently swoops off, noisy as can be, their black shapes covering the blue sky with ever-changing patterns.

There is a waiting quality in the air. All the world is waiting for the really chilly weather of November. These last few warm days are to be appreciated. All those gardens as yet untouched by frost are in their height of bloom. The flowers are spectacular in all their tawny shades, with gold predominating. The ageratum seems to have caught the blueness from the shadows. My volunteer alyssum grows up out of the flagstone cracks into snowy, white cushions.

I am sitting on the terrace watching the leaves fall. I have a handsome tree at the edge of the bank—a chokecherry. Most of its leaves are still green, but autumn has gilded some, and now and then, when a little whiff of breeze comes, one or three or seven fall—gold leaves on the very green grass below. There is nothing more peaceful than sitting quietly alone watching leaves fall. Some drift and float this way and that on their route to earth; some plummet straight down. They rather resemble us going through our lives. Some of us move straight toward a goal; some turn in a variety of directions, quite like a falling leaf, following an assortment of avenues through life.

I am sitting here alone, experiencing and appreciating the special joys of solitude. My neighbors are not out. I enjoy it when they are, and we exchange greetings. But I also cherish a time alone. When you are alone outdoors you are never really alone. You blend with your environment, not losing anything in your aloneness, but gaining a sense of wholeness, a wholeness with everything, a sense of oneness with being. Body, mind, and spirit are all for a brief time one, poised in a moment of eternity.

We come nearer to the inner self when we are alone. We get better acquainted with ourselves. If you are a stranger to yourself, you are a stranger to other people. When you are connected with your own deep center you are then enabled to connect with the deep center of another human being.

We all need some time alone—short intervals during the day, longer intervals during the week, and occasionally a few days alone. Solitude alternating with companionship, withdrawal alternating with return, is what keeps us at peace with ourselves. What with radio and television, some of us live with a lot of noise until it becomes essential to us. When the noise stops, there needs to be some "inner music" to take its place. Perhaps we must learn over again how to let our inner music emerge.

Solitude is so different from loneliness. Solitude is a state of peace and rest. Loneliness is a restless seeking for something you can't identify. Loneliness is also an overinvolvement with the self.

In a few minutes I will go over to the Center to catch the bus to the symphony in Philadelphia. I will enjoy my friends on the bus, as well as the music once we get there. I will enjoy it more for having had my time of solitude here first. Interludes of solitude between events cause you to appreciate each event more. I am thinking of the music I will hear. Today I am rich. I will have had both kinds of music—inner music and outer.

What a dreamy afternoon yesterday was. It is so pleasant to sit in the Academy of Music in the dim light and hear all those magnificent melodies. Our prologue came on the drive in, with lovely, colored foliage lining the sides of the roads. There seems to me to be a direct relationship between nature and music. There is lyricism in the roads we travel these days, with red and gold, bronze and copper leaves, and now and then a gold maple backlit by the sun. There is a rhythm in all the colors we see over the landscape, in the broad, rolling fields with their waving, tan grass, in the arrangement of fences marking them off, in the Pennsylvania stone houses along the way.

This morning I noticed that one of my bronze chrysanthemums was wilting, some of the flower heads drooping in a dejected way. I ran the hose on them. Two hours later the bronze flowers were all perked up. Nothing is more responsive than a garden, and it is satisfying to be responded to so promptly. We love people who respond to us, and likewise do we love our gardens when they respond. That is one of the delights of gardening. You cultivate a row of beans, and the next day it looks different from the beets you didn't cultivate. So, promptly you cultivate the beets, and soon they, too, respond.

When you have this ready response, you feel related to the garden and all in it, just as you relate closely to a friend when he or she responds to you in a conversation.

I don't know what people who don't have gardens do. How much they miss. This quick response is one thing that endears gardening to me. My little terrace garden is a joy. It is visible from my living room and my bedroom. When I close my window in the morning I take a long and loving look. The chrysanthemum garden is right outside the bedroom window.

When I look at my African violets in the window with the sun shining on them I think they are my favorite flowers. Then I go out to look at the chrysanthemums and know that *they* are my favorites!

Today I had lunch out by these chrysanthemums. With the last tomatoes from my garden I made tomato and cottage cheese salad. Occasionally a few leaves floated down on me when a little gust of wind came my way. The trees across the valley were radiant. This is the day when I am sure fall is my favorite time of year and October my favorite month.

This afternoon I had a delightful swim. I always meet a few friends at the pool, and they make pleasant company as I swim back and forth the pool's length. I do eight round trips, an eighth of a mile. Sometimes I don't bother to count, but just relax and swim. It seems to me that swimming is a perfect pastime. Stretching out in the water makes me feel so good.

After my swim I went down to the vegetable garden and picked raspberries. I will ask Edith to have dinner with me, and we'll come back to my apartment for dessert.

I love picking raspberries. The feel of each berry as it falls in my hand is a pleasure. And of course I have to eat a few as I go along. With powdered sugar and cream they will be a delight tonight.

The color across my valley is at its height. I think this same thought every day. Yet I am sure that it is so now, this minute. Leaves are blowing, the whole world sparkles. When you drive anywhere in the car, you see wild grape leaves turned gold, festooning small trees and bushes along the roadside. Gold leaves swirl around the car and along the pavement before you. Nature is in her full glory. I am going to keep this moment in time, treasure it, and bring it out next January when the world is all white and the snow sifts down.

What a lovely party! A couple at Crosslands decided to give a party for everyone here—a dance in the auditorium. It was a beautiful occasion: a fine orchestra, candlelight, a great full moon shining in the window, and everyone all dressed up and in a party mood.

We were drawn out of our usual selves, all of us, I think. Gaiety and laughter was everywhere. A side of us that we don't usually meet comes to the fore on such occasions. For a few hours we flow with the music, dance, sip punch, and eat crisp cookies. Everyone is warm and responsive. We have small exchanges with our friends.

We should do this more often, everyone says, but we all know that these occasions are perhaps especially meaningful because they don't come too often. But when they do come, how we all cherish them.

I am sitting on my terrace sewing. Sally's garden, three apartments away, is so colorful I will go over and see it more closely. Sally is out working in it. I have such nice neighbors. Sally and I converse a while, then she comes back to see my garden. We are looking at it when Frank comes out with his camera to get some color pictures of the gardens. Frank and Emily are my next-door neighbors to the right. And now Norma, my next-door neighbor to the left, emerges to water her flowers. She joins the conversation.

How lucky I am to live here, where the neighbors are so pleasant and friendly. You can never be lonely in this atmosphere, and yet I also have the solitude I cherish. Many are the mornings when I sit on my terrace for two hours and never see a soul. I live in both worlds, and it is ideal.

I woke to the sound of rain on the terrace. Looking out the window, I could see the branches of the cherry tree and my little weeping birch dancing madly in the wind while the rain blew up the valley in sheets.

This is the first real rain we have had since June. There were just a few brief showers during the summer. I think you feel sort of tight inside during a prolonged drought. But now, in this heavenly rain, I feel relaxed again. I hope it goes on and on, for all day at least. It is a good day to answer letters and read, the kind of day your umbrella blows inside out in the wind. I will stay in.

I keep looking out the window to be sure it is still raining. You can feel with the plants and trees the beneficence of the rain.

The month draws to a close. With Jane I took a drive past frosted corn fields, gold and tan in the sunlight. Black and white cows are grazing in green fields, and three crows are calling. A golden tulip tree reaches up toward a black thunderhead. Through the woods tall pines are splashed through with gold here and there, and the sunlight filters down.

Later, I took a walk down by the woods, scuffing through ankle-deep dry leaves. Is it raining? No, those are leaves falling—yellow tulip leaves, crunchy, gold maple leaves, and all the others. The trees are letting go of that which they do not want or need anymore. Can I do the same?

2 ❈

November Is Appreciating

November comes sweeping up the valley in a chilly wind. Each night lately we have had a frost, and the grass is dusted white early in the morning. The terrace garden has survived until last night: The chrysanthemums, marigolds, and alyssum are still in fine shape, but many annuals were frosted and limp this morning. I had an interesting time pulling out all these dead plants. The basic planting of yews, mugho pines, birds nest spruce, dwarf alberta spruce, hollies, hanoki cypress, and prostrate juniper was all but crowded out of sight by the annuals. As I pulled these up, it was rather like sculpting; I brought back into being the basic design of the garden. When I finished, I sat on the terrace a few minutes and admired the original plan Mr. Manni had done for me, which is now clearly visible.

These days I have a persistent and very pleasant vision of the sap running down inside the branches and tree trunks to settle in the roots. Here I picture it sliding down for the next few months, replenishing itself in preparation for the great uprush of spring. A biologist might take exception to my vision. But I really don't want to be corrected. I enjoy my concept because it seems to symbolize what happens in human areas too.

As the weather chills and crisps, we spend more and more days settled in indoor activities. This is also the time our thinking and feeling centers quicken. As we slip into these inward parts of us, we are alert to bits of philosophy we read and hear. We are ready to make these a part of our daily thinking and meditation. Winter can be an inward renewal: Our spirits stir and waken. We feel new growing pains, and we grasp and absorb fresh concepts. The spirit of all living develops and evolves within.

We are at the gateway of winter and inward renewal.

This morning I went to the supermarket. The drive down past all the colorful leaves on Route 52 was dramatic. Although many leaves have fallen, a great quantity are still left. There is a huge maple at the corner of 52 and Route 1 that is half deep apricot and half still green. The tree was so diverting, I had to concentrate on paying attention to the road. The sumac bushes, which a few weeks ago unobtrusively faded into the general greenness, are now flamboyant fringes of scarlet. And bittersweet trails its orange berries over bushes along the roadside. Something in me sang.

I parked in the large lot outside the Acme, chose my wire cart, and went through the automatic doors. Something inside me was still singing, especially when I saw the long counters of fresh fruit and vegetables. They are really beautiful. Yes, I mean beautiful—the rows of oranges, grapefruit, pears, pineapples, carrots, lettuce, green peppers, grapes, and bananas. I was filled with admiration and in a pleasant glow as I picked out some pears.

I was remembering some months ago when I was in the Acme in just such a mood. The woman next to me was speaking.

"It's such a bore to shop, I just hate it. Don't you?"

"Oh," I said, taken aback. "Well, you see, I've been in bed with the flu, and this is my first time out, so I am feeling rather good to be able to be here."

She gave me a stony look as she continued to pick out oranges.

Today, no such person spoke to me. The man who weighs the fruit was humming to himself as he arranged a pile of honeydew melons. How lovely they looked too, firm, and white, and round.

I felt a hint of guilt that I hadn't been more sympathetic to the woman who spoke a few months back. I wasn't very understanding, and many is the day when I have been low-spirited and nothing throws me lower than a *very* cheerful person. Oh hum, well that's water over the dam now, today, and I do feel wonderful.

Across the aisle was a very attractive young woman carrying a sleeping baby, the tiniest I have ever seen. I walked over.

"What an adorable baby," I said. The woman looked at me. She could be no more than seventeen. I asked the name of the baby.

"Donna," she said. "She is just five days old, and I am on the way home from the hospital. My husband has half of my list."

The baby yawned and then slept on.

I thought of what a great adventure they were embarking on.

When I paid for my groceries and the woman handed me my change, she looked up smiling.

"Have a good day," she said.

Traveling home on Route 1 was just as pleasant as the trip in had been. Here and there scarlet dogwood bordered the road. There is something so stirring about these fall days. It is as if nature were feeling a sort of recklessness and having a last fling with her whole palette of colors over the landscape. Pushing aside all thoughts of winter to come, you live in the now, absorbing the glory on all sides. Today winter is eons away and so is anything difficult or unpleasant. The world is sunny and smiling.

Back at Crosslands, I stopped for my mail and got a nice letter from Delbert, my brother-in-law, on Cape Cod. He and Kay would meet my plane when I go for a visit later in the month. I am going to spend Thanksgiving at Nauset Heights in their delightful house that looks out over the Atlantic Ocean, the beach, and breaking waves. Nothing lies between them and Spain.

November is the month of traveling seedpods that eagerly reach out to touch and cling to your skirt or stocking, pants or jacket. They are filled with wanderlust and want to be taken to a new spot to call home where they can root and grow.

How pleasant was my dessert party last night. There were eight of us (eight is the number that fits into my living room). We women all wore long dresses. This was to celebrate autumn. It was fun to see everyone in gala mood and dress. After eating dinner at the Center, we came back to my apartment and ate the snow pudding and custard sauce I had made in the morning. It was a gay party. Everyone was relaxed and happy, and we all exchanged ideas for a time. Then everyone went home. I did the dishes, ruminating on all that had been said and on how nice everyone had looked.

It is good to have a party now and then. Entertaining friends is always a pleasure. I like to cook and to make desserts especially. My guests were nostalgic about the snow pudding of their childhood as they ate mine tonight.

If a leaf falls from a tree between you and the sun, its dark blue shadow runs over the ground from where you stand to meet the leaf as it lands.

Watch next time and see.

Many November days are gray days, the sky covered with heavy silver-gray clouds. Here and there comes a break in the clouds and a shaft of sunlight catches and lights up an occasional remaining gold maple or red dogwood.

This is the season of dramatic sunsets, startling brilliant gold and gray and violet skies, with a smoky orange afterglow. The days are getting shorter, and if I drive with a friend to my favorite sunset-viewing hilltop, I must go around five o'clock to catch the sun going down.

From time to time we all have a need for a new person in our lives, a new experience, a new encounter, a drive somewhere interesting, a dessert party, a symphony. Something that lifts the day above the ordinary is as important as air and sunlight. It makes one see things anew and freshly. It lends a touch of magic to the week, the day, the hour. Life can become extremely routine if you let it; one must ascend a peak now and then.

Something we all need and I always try to have are goals—plenty of goals, large goals, small goals, near goals, and distant goals. Something to look forward to, something to plan for. Perhaps a party, a small trip somewhere, or a larger trip—all these are stimulating and enriching.

My nearest goal at the moment is to have Bob and Esther over for fresh cider and snacks at four-thirty today before we three eat dinner together at the Center. Tomorrow, Francis Hall comes here to lead a seminar on "The Spiritual Life in Retirement Years." That will be an enriching experience. One of my most exciting goals is my trip to Cape Cod, which comes up later this month. I'm beginning to plan what I will take and what I will leave behind. My distant goal is a trip in February to Tryon, North Carolina, where I lived before I came here. I've arranged for a little house there. I've loads of friends in Tryon. It is a lot warmer there than here, and all in all it will be a wonderful experience.

Today is so cold. I'm sure I was never this cold in November before. A wild and chilly wind is blowing and taking the last leaves off the trees. I was well bundled up when I took my mile walk around the circle this morning. I must be getting older to be so chilly. But I already *am* older. Oh hum. I'll have to make my peace with winter some way, and soon. All the same, it will be nice to be somewhere warmer for February at least, and it will be a real joy to see my friends again.

Being with people you enjoy is a delight. We need to do this often; but it is equally vital to be with people who *enjoy you*. Somehow you sense this, and it fills your sails and carries you on forward.

It is important to seek your true self. You probably never find it in the sense of being able to define it; but in relationships we get a few clues. You will never find your true self if you go out of your way looking for it; but as you relate to another or others you get a sense of your true dimension.

How can you ever define this true self when it is unlimited, ever-changing, and a good bit larger than any finite image you may glimpse? But in a relationship, glimpse by glimpse, you can get a feel of yourself as you really are. Perhaps we need to be content with this.

Ourselves "as we really are" is ever-changing, too, as we grow a little. And through relationships we grow—more if the relationship is from deep center to deep center, less if it is from surface to surface.

People laugh at the old comment "How do I know what I think until I hear what I say?" However, this is something to pause over and consider. What comes out spontaneously in conversation with another or in a group reveals bits of your true self if you are alert enough to catch them.

November is the month of Thanksgiving, giving thanks and appreciation. How important it is for us all to remember to express the appreciation we feel for our friends *and* for ourselves.

We all need praise and appreciation. The more we are appreciated, the more we become worth appreciating, the more our self-confidence soars.

Will I ever feel secure enough not to need some praise as I go along through life? I doubt it. Will anyone? The human being, if normal, needs to be praised and appreciated all through life, especially when growing up, and again particularly when older. And of course in between—always.

We so often think complimentary things about another, a family member for instance, but we usually forget to express them. A simple way of making someone feel really good is to tell him something complimentary that you have never verbalized before. And of course appreciation is also very important when it comes to ourselves. Half the time, we don't even bother to like ourselves. We need to think highly of ourselves.

Not only do we need to appreciate each other and ourselves, but this should also include things, places, weather, life, everything. We coast along for a few days or a week and overlook the fact that it is a very special time. Yet we look back and think how happy we were during that period. Do we remember to appreciate where we live, our views from the windows, our gardens, our neighbors?

Perhaps this is the message of November—to appreciate everything worth appreciating in your life and every person you know and like, even some you don't like. Knowing people you don't like can be a growing experience.

In nearly every situation there is something to praise and find joy in. If we remember to do this, we will enrich our days, our weeks, our years, and ourselves. And we will have received the message life sends us through the month of November.

When the great change occurs in nature and the last leaf has fallen, you see the bare bones of the tree, you see its basic structure. Perhaps when a big change comes about in our lives we, too, as we cope, reveal what we inwardly are.

This is the season when the Canada geese in my area gather together in great flocks and head south. It is fascinating to see their large numbers almost covering the sky, in several vast V's as they prepare for their departure. We have many of them on our pond and a few different flocks flying about all summer. But at this season the young, hatched and raised in the pond, are grown, and immense families of them all come together for the long trip ahead. Some groups remain because there are ponds over at Longwood Gardens and they like it there. But yesterday I saw the largest number I had yet seen. Necks outstretched, they were soaring southward through the blue heavens.

They make such a haunting noise when they fly. They must be communicating something—what, I often wonder. What sort of things do they say to each other? Unanswerable question! Nonetheless, one I often ponder.

Some of the chrysanthemums have been killed by recent frosts, so I cut them back. They were so fragrant—the leaves and stalks. And after my hands touched them they, too, were fragrant. It is one of the last garden smells of the season.

In fall all outdoors has a wonderful scent. You notice it after you have been inside a couple of hours or when you first go out in the morning. It is a mix of rich autumn earth, dried crushed leaves, and wood smoke. It's not a bit like outdoor smells in spring. Each season has its special odors, and this pungent fall fragrance is especially welcome and wonderful.

Francis Hall left by plane this morning, after our seminar on "The Spiritual Life in Retirement Years." Our meetings were held in the guest house here called Ellerslie. Each day he led us in a workshop. We had discussions and experiences, and all together it was a rich and rewarding few days. There were twenty-one of us, a good size. Now today, with it all over, I feel still slightly out of this world. It is difficult to settle into anything, and I don't try very hard. I just drifted through today. I did get my suitcase out and began packing for the Cape. But that is all.

We've had a couple of days of a wild wind, and a cold one, and now a day I call dismal – gray and cold and ominous. I walked around the circle well wrapped with a heavy wool scarf around my neck, winter coat, and mittens. It was twenty-five degrees last night. Jane came over, and we covered the chrysanthemums first with leaves and then hay from the garden. I put the plastic covers on the terrace chairs and tables. And now I know winter is here. Jane and I sat in the warm cozy living room and sipped lovely fresh cider. Then I noticed it was snowing. Just casual, drifting flakes few and far between at first. Presently they became more businesslike. By four-thirty it began to get dark, and by dinnertime there was a light dusting of snow on our lawns and roofs and it was raining.

It makes me a little nervous to think of flying in this weather. But surely by Thursday it will be over. I am sending up a little prayer. I do want to get to Cape Cod on schedule. I am nearly all packed and prepared. I am fitting nicely into the one not-too-large suitcase.

Here I am in Kay and Del's house on the bluff overlooking the beach and the Atlantic Ocean. The sun is streaming down, the sea a deep, deep blue. The wind is blowing the wild roses and barberry outside the windows. How good it is to be back here again. We are all so congenial and get on so well together. Del has a fire laid and, as it began to get dark, he lit it. The sparks flew up the chimney while flames darted among them. We sat and watched the fire and talked and caught up on each other's news. Crosslands seemed miles and miles away as we ate fresh lobster dipped in melted butter by the fire with candlelight and soft music. The smell of the fire filled the room. The wind blew in the chimney. We could hear the sound of the breakers on the beach, and I was deeply content.

How exhilarating it is standing beside the sea watching the waves break. How good you feel. Here by the ocean you have a sense that you are a part of all creation. Just wandering down to the beach and to the brink of the sea has been invigorating. In a strange sort of way it all—the vast expanse of sky, the sand, the sea, yes, and the shore birds as well—seems to belong to you and you to them. You feel you have had a hand in making them all, a hand in all creation.

No need to take a picture. No need to refer to an album. The beauty is all in the mind's eye, in our hearts and souls. It becomes ours and in a way we can never lose it.

There is something important that has come to me as a realization lately. We three have been talking about it. It is about eras. Our lives are made up of a series of periods. Certain things—the furniture of your life and your location—belong to certain eras and not to others.

My husband and I had lived in Connecticut and reveled in snow and winters and a place six acres large with a huge organic vegetable garden, a stream, a meadow of wildflowers, a woodland with a primrose path through it, and a greenhouse with seventy-five orchid plants in it. We were many miles from the nearest store-bought carrot or a quart of milk, and it didn't matter. Gradually we moved from the time when that was all perfect to the time when it didn't fit so well. We had passed into a new period, and that place was no longer ideal. We moved to Tryon, North Carolina, to a smaller house, no greenhouse, no vegetable garden. We had a charmed bit of woodland and a stream. We were one mile from all the stores. This perfectly fit our new era and continued to do so for a number of years. We were absolutely happy there. Then my husband died, and I stepped into still another era, and the Tryon house no longer belonged to the new stage I was in.

It was at this time that I moved to Crosslands. One thing that followed me throughout these stages was a stream. One in Connecticut, one in Tryon, and now the superb view from my terrace includes a brook in the valley.

The tendency we all have is to cling to a previous era and try to feel we belong there, and that some of the "furnishings" of the previous era belong with us still. But they really don't. It is difficult to let go of certain periods in our lives. We are wise if we can let go of all that belongs to a previous time when we leave it.

A resident at Crosslands built a small greenhouse outside his apartment where he raises orchids. That's just what I'll do, I thought when I first saw it. Then I thought about it for a bit and realized that orchids were part of the furnishings of a previous era of mine. I am no longer in that period, I told myself firmly, and I resisted the greenhouse and the orchids. I am very happy with neither.

You must put your mind and heart and soul into the era you are in—to be there with all of you.

Kay and Del and I had some wonderful discussions of eras and what belonged in which one and where we all were.

Something significant happened to me tonight. Kay and I were listening to the Boston Symphony on television. They were playing Brahms's Fourth Symphony. All at once I realized I was enjoying it enormously. I was really carried away by it. Then I became aware that this was an important moment. Together, my husband, Bob, and I had first heard this piece of music some years ago at the New York Symphony. We then got the record and played it a great deal. It was one of our favorites. After Bob died, whenever I heard it I was sad and nostalgic. I never *could* play the record. This was the way with many mutual joys. I remembered, and it was painful. I remembered with sadness and longing. But tonight I had listened and remembered with great pleasure *because it was* something we did together.

Then I became aware that gradually over these last few years, without realizing it, I had changed. I could remember some mutual joy or pastime, some mutual activity, or just anything about Bob, now, with joy, not grief. Will this always be true from now on? It just might be. Tonight was a milestone.

Thanksgiving lasted three days with the three of us there on the bluff. First, before dinner, my nephew and his family gave a party where we all sang Thanksgiving songs. My nephew gave a moving Thanksgiving prayer, and we had a gay time. A favorite grandson of mine arrived and we had a turkey dinner with all the flourishes—cranberry sauce, apple pie, and such. We ate by a beautiful grate fire. What a gala time! I sat up late by the fire talking with my grandson.

Next day, Joan, my daughter, arrived from Boston. We walked on the beach and saw hundreds of gulls and sandpipers. A fire is just part of our lives these cold days, and we four sat by it and talked and talked. She and I sat up late exchanging ideas, and she stayed through the next day.

What a rewarding Thanksgiving! We had a real family time. The ties of family are strong, and on Thanksgiving you realize how strong.

I was eating my sandwich in the airport in Hyannis, waiting for the plane for Boston, the first leg of my journey to Philadelphia. Pretty soon they called the departure and I walked toward the plane. It was so windy I didn't see why that small plane wasn't blown across the runway.

It seemed smaller than when I had taken it coming down two weeks before. I got in, as did about ten other people. As we lifted off the ground the wind tossed the little plane like a blowing leaf, and we were nearly bounced out of our seats. The pilot assured us that, although the wind was strong and it would be rough, we were quite safe. "Just bear with it and roll with the punches," he said. I held onto my seat and hoped I looked better than I felt. I was scared to death. If I ever land from this flight, I told myself, it will be a long, long time before I get into another small plane.

Why didn't the wind turn the little plane over, I wondered, as I looked down at the sea below and saw the great white caps and huge breakers roll up on the sands. Perhaps it would before we arrived.

"No cause for alarm," the pilot said again through the loud-speaker as the plane lurched to one side. This went on and on, and the breakers below grew wilder, and the water was white with foam.

If I landed in the sea, I speculated, would it be better to take off my fur coat lest its weight sink me, or would it even when wet keep me warm, and would it ever be the same again? Would I? I was wondering about these things when a terrific lurch threw us all over to the left. Perhaps by the time I had that decision to make about my coat I'd be dead, I thought, holding the arm of the seat firmly. Even with a seat belt, I didn't feel secure.

With a vast, relieved sigh I felt the ground in Boston beneath the plane wheels. I felt as if I had been given a new life. How beautiful the runway looked, and the airport was a palace!

As I stood in the airport, the message of November came clear and loud, and I found myself appreciating being alive.

3❀

December Is Giving

December came stealing over the landscape in a silent snow-fall—a gentle, light snow that dusted the grass and bushes and left the roads intact after a few cars had been over them. By daylight it cleared and the sun rose.

When I returned to Crosslands from Cape Cod I found two weeks of mail waiting: a number of letters from friends, which were welcome, a marathon letter from my son Bob. He doesn't write often, but when he does he writes a volume, and I love it.

Also awaiting me were the galleys of my new book, *The Touch of the Earth*. I had a pleasant few days going over them. I enjoyed reading the book again. Having a book coming out is an exciting experience to look forward to. It involves so many fine moments. The acceptance of the project is of course a peak experience; signing the contract is also exciting. Communicating with your editor, approving the cuts, seeing the jacket drawing for the first time, receiving the galleys, seeing the finished books, reading the reviews, getting letters from readers—all these are momentous occasions. *The Touch of the Earth* is now off to press, and I've nothing more to do with it until it comes out.

I am sitting in the dazzling sunlight in my living room. It is pouring across the room, filling the whole place with light. It is so cheerful and delightful. It is cold out—in the twenties, so I am pleased to be settled where it is warm and cozy.

As I sit here I am thinking about December and what it has to tell us. December is the month of giving—giving and receiving. We sit down to write Christmas cards and we give our thoughts and affection to each person we send a card to. We go to pick up the mail and we receive cards from faraway places and faraway people—perhaps those we hear from only once a year. It is rewarding to be linked with far-off friends by a gay and cheery card and message.

Mysterious packages arrive from family and close friends. It is all such fun, these outward aspects of this annual holiday. Or are they outward aspects? Not exclusively. Many a deep thought and something to ponder comes to me on a Christmas card. And how much thought and love goes into picking out a Christmas present!

Then, there is the still-deeper side of Christmas, the giving on a deeper level.

It is interesting to realize that a tree is not depleted by scattering its seed. It is fulfilled. Likewise, we do not become less by giving but more as we also are fulfilled. The more we give ourselves away the more is there to give. And this is the season of special giving. But giving is in no way limited to December. In fact, I think it is good to give a friend a present just because you think of something that person would like or needs—no Christmas or birthday involved. Giving is just plain fun. Giving of yourself leaves you feeling deeply content. Perhaps our message from December is to give, on all levels, at any time of year.

December nights are clear and crisp and the stars sparkle. They would be perfect for stargazing if only it weren't so cold. You can't very well lie on your back on a blanket on the grass and pick out Cassiopeia, Pegasus, Aquila, Delphinus, and others the way you can in August. And in August it isn't as clear. The stars these nights are best viewed out the window. When I lie in bed the bare-branched cherry tree outside my window seems spangled with stars. As the breeze stirs the branches, they first conceal and then reveal stars, and this causes the stars themselves to twinkle merrily.

Did you ever look at the center of a poinsettia blossom? It is fascinating. It is composed of a cluster of buds, furry at the top. Every bud has at the side and near the top a tiny tube, sometimes two. As the bloom matures, this tube not only turns gold, but opens to hold a drop of clear liquid. When Christmas comes again, study a poinsettia center. It will be well worth your while.

I was in Heritage Gardens Nursery yesterday and I fell in love with a very small and healthy-looking poinsettia plant with a single, huge bloom on it. It was pink, just the shade that looks lovely in my living room, with its light green walls and blue-green chair covers and tan sofa. So home it went with me to be ceremoniously placed on the table by the sofa, where its lovely pink shade goes so well with the lavender sofa cushions. It is just the right size for my apartment.

"Oh Little Town of Bethlehem" is among my favorite carols. So is "Noel" and "Silent Night." We sang them all at the concert this afternoon. There was an hour of Christmas music in the auditorium, and it was beautiful. An instrumental ensemble played, a choral group sang, and at times the audience sang too. How close you feel to those with whom you sing carols! It was Christmas in essence. I love to sing carols at this time of year, especially in a group. I don't sing very well, but if I am in a group and those around me are singing loudly, I find the courage to sing. Then, if I am off key it isn't so evident! Everyone was in such a good mood when it was over: smiles everywhere and cheerful good wishes. Christmas is ahead a bit, but the spirit of it is already evident.

I mailed all my cards today, and this gave me a good feeling. I enjoy writing them with a special message to each person, and I enjoy receiving them. There are so many friends I hear from just once a year! But it is meaningful when I do hear. This is a warm and wonderful season.

I went over to Heritage Gardens again this morning. There was a pleasant hustle and bustle there. Pine and cedar roping lay in coils on the floor, and an assortment of beautiful and fragrant wreaths were scattered about. There were bunches of holly, pine boughs, pine cones, hemlock wreaths, and branches of mixed evergreens for hanging on doors. Such a glorious variety of greens and scents. A kind of holiday magic filled the air.

I bought a Christmas wreath for my door—a lovely balsam one that smelled wonderful. It turned my apartment into an Adirondak forest while I was arranging a few pine cones on it and a nice red bow. It hangs in the hall on my apartment door now, and whenever I go in or out I take a deep breath of a pungent woodland scent.

With my poinsettia and my wreath I was feeling well decorated when I got an intriguing package from John in Tryon. Inside was a delft bowl with planted crocuses already in great fat buds. The jar has holes in the side and more crocuses growing out of them. All I need now are a few pine boughs for the top of the desk where I shall put my little, tin, Mexican Christmas tree. I'll put pine branches on the table, too. I can get them from the woods nearby. I love the fragrances of Christmas.

It is very cold today. The rhododendron leaves are curled up like small green cigars. But it seems the day to get pine branches, so Jane and I put on sweaters and warm coats and head off in the car to cut some. The pine woodland we discover is fragrant and the ground is covered with scented needles. We fill our basket with small branches and start for home. What a pleasure to arrange my branches on top of the desk and in the center of my dining table. On top of the desk I spread pine branches, a few pine cones, and some red berries. I also place there two very fat candles that I have had for years and always burn at Christmas. In the center of the arrangement I put the little tin Christmas tree from Mexico with charming designs painted on it. At the tip of each tin branch is a candle holder, seven in all, and I set a red candle in each one.

Mark and Fran came for dinner last night and brought beach plum jelly and the most glorious red azalea plant with festoons of flowers already open and many buds to watch unfold the next few weeks. The azalea adds to my living-room Christmas garden. The crocuses now have little tufts of green at the tip of each bud, promises of flowers to come.

My philodendron and shamrock form a nice background for these special plants. The African violets add glamor to the scene. The leaves I potted in October are flourishing, but show no sign of new growth yet.

After dinner we went over to Longwood Gardens to a Christmas concert. The conservatories were filled with poinsettias—red, white, and pink—and the flowers were enormous. There were also large Christmas trees decorated by different garden clubs. Each one added a touch of fairyland. The concert was beautiful, and we all sang carols. The decorations were festive and fabulous. We had a memorable evening.

I had returned from dinner and was sitting alone in my living room thinking about the friends whose cards I had just opened. I began remembering last Christmas, the joys, and then the problem of having my purse stolen, and I was thinking perhaps I'd better lock my terrace door because there were sinister influences abroad now.

It was then that I first heard them, the carol singers—way off in the distance. Was it someone's radio? No, it was real. A long way off I heard "Joy to the World." The music grew louder and louder as it neared. I opened my door to the hall and there they were, a miscellaneous group of people, mostly teenagers in jeans and sweaters, a few grownups, a few children—all were singing. Now it was "Oh Little Town of Bethlehem" as they approached down the hall. It was so beautiful, so unexpected, such a surprise. I stood rooted to the spot while they all came along smiling and greeting me. Other residents had opened their doors, too. The group then slipped into "Silent Night" as they passed my door. Gradually the music faded as they moved on out the door into the night.

I had been *thinking* a lot about Christmas lately and what it meant to me, and all of a sudden, while I stood watching the young people and hearing them sing, I began to *feel* Christmas, and I was filled with a warm and wonderful sensation of relating to all people everywhere. It was a moving experience. When they had left and all was quiet again, there was still a warm glow within me; it lasted all evening, and is even with me now, the next morning.

This morning I learned that it was the First Baptist Church of Kennett Square that entertained us so beautifully, that had switched my mood from one of fear to one of love.

This brings me back to December being the month of giving. Here were these young people from the church giving their time and enthusiasm on a very cold winter night to sing carols all through Crosslands, thus giving pleasure to so many.

There is a feeling of caring abroad these days, too. The feeling is in the air. When I went shopping today it was the same in the stores. There was a feeling of everyone being your friend and neighbor in the best sense of the words. At Christmas time there is a great feeling of oneness permeating the very air we breathe. This is a feeling we'd like to hold onto for the rest of the year. But it is a feeling that waxes and wanes, goes up and down, and at Christmas time it reaches the wave crest – the peak. This feeling stays with us for several days. With me, it begins to mount about the middle of December and reaches its climax on Christmas Day itself, and then slowly recedes. It is not that we stop being neighborly; but there is a different sense of it. No wave reaches its crest to remain there. It breaks and goes into a trough before it builds up to the next crest. So it is with us; our feelings ebb and flow, and Christmas is a time of year when there is a special flow.

Christmas means many things to many people. One meaning it has for me is: Find and follow your star and it will lead you to treasure that will change your world.

I woke to a temperature of six degrees – brilliant sunshine through my living room, and plenty of wind blowing the trees outside. It was so cold walking over to the Center for dinner, but the chilliness and wind were amply compensated for by the warm and cheery greetings from everyone. The Christmas decorations at the Center were lovely. There were several great wreaths of balsam with touches of heather and large yellow bows—all so fragrant. A lovely decorated tree stood outside the building, and there was one in the dining room charmingly decorated with festoons of silver tinsel and tiny lights.

As planned, I ate dinner with Esther and Bob and Elizabeth. We had a round table in the corner of the small room. Every table had pieces of holly in the center. Large white paper snowflakes hung from the chandeliers. What a marvelous meal we had: the best turkey I have ever eaten, and all that goes with it, winding up with hot mince pie and vanilla ice cream.

This afternoon I am filled with peace and joy. I have just read over all my Christmas cards, and so many people have wished me peace and joy I just have to be filled with both, and I am. I am, indeed, feeling very content and happy. It is good to hear from so many people from places far and near and read their messages and notes. Now and then there was a family letter telling of the year's activities. These were most interesting.

Christmas is a very special time of year and a very special day. You think warm and loving thoughts of friends everywhere, and you always have a vast circle of those who are very dear.

While I am sitting here thinking of the deeper meanings of Christmas, the phone rings and my son Bob, his wife, Susan, and their two sons are on the wire. We have a lovely talk. They are skiing in Squaw Valley in the West, and practically breathed over the phone of ski slopes and open spaces. I could just picture the skiers with their gay jackets and scarves and mittens flying down the slopes in great swooping curves. It took me back many years to when my husband, Bob, and I went skiing winters in New England and the children, just youngsters then, came with us.

After a while the phone rings again, and my other son, Tim, his wife, Jeanne, and their two young people are on the line. It is so heart-warming to hear their voices and learn what they have been doing. Through the everyday things we talk about over such a great distance come the deeper feelings we all have for each other.

I often wonder what people do who don't have children. They mean so much to you all their lives and yours, and when you get older their calls and letters are especially heart-warming.

The temperature was five degrees this morning. The roads are icy. Our walkways are cleared, but the open walks are still icy. Everywhere is brilliant sunshine, and my apartment is bathed in it.

Today is a good day to bake bread, I decide. I love to bake bread. And I like to make a lot this time of year and give warm loaves to friends and neighbors. It takes all morning to bake; four loaves is what comes out of my recipe, two large and two small. So at lunchtime I am delivering bread. I took one loaf to Frances this afternoon at about four, and she asked me in for tea. Giving fresh bread is such a pleasant thing to do. Each loaf I deliver evolves into a visit. Everyone is so welcoming. And, of course, while the bread bakes the apartment smells wonderful. So altogether I had a fine day. What a good way to spend the time when you are iced in! I believe I will bake more tomorrow. Then I will have made twelve loaves this week and given one to just about everyone I had in mind.

Today began with a heavy mist. I cannot see across the valley. And the trees on our side are a sort of hazy blur. I started the day with a swim in our lovely pool here. Our pool is like a small tropic. There are a great number of plants in the room around the edges. It is so warm you think you are in the jungle. There are camellias, ferns, ivies, huge philodendrons, and many other varieties. When I returned to my apartment I found a corrugated box outside my door. I took it in, and there was an amaryllis bulb, all potted and ready to grow. I have never seen such a large one before. If its flowers are in proportion to the bulb, it will fill the living room. A friend brought it to me. What a lovely thought. My living room turns more and more into a garden.

I feel ever so much more at home here in Crosslands this year. I believe it has taken me three years to feel that I belong here. This has been a very large adjustment to make coming just when I was in the process of making the adjustment to living without my husband. Community living like this is so different from living in your own house in a small town. You are in constant touch with so many people whom you know just slightly. Of course, there are a few whom you know better all the time.

Living here is constant practice in relating to people, both those you know slightly and those you know better. We are each independent, with our own apartments, each one like a little house. Still, we are also part of a community and are constantly aware of this.

I love to dance. We had a masquerade ball here tonight, New Year's Eve. The auditorium was handsomely decorated with hundreds of balloons and festoons of colored paper streamers. There was an amusing skit first, and then a parade of those in costume, and then dancing. It was from seven-thirty to ten, which is the "Quaker midnight." Just before "midnight," the old year came in and walked around a bit. He was enveloped in a large, white sheet and wore a long, white, cotton beard, and he carried a fierce-looking scythe! When he went out, the new year came dancing in. The smallest of the residents, dressed as a child, skipped around the room. Everyone clapped; the balloons swayed. Everyone was wishing everyone a Happy New Year. It was a gala moment and a gala occasion. A wonderful evening.

When I got back to my apartment I lit the candles on my little tin Christmas tree and the other two fat candles on the desk and sat here in my "garden" hooking my rug and thinking over the fun of the evening.

As the year draws to a close, it seems the time to look back as well as ahead.

What was the shape of the year that just passed? It had its high moments and a few low ones, as always happens. The months past have had many rewarding experiences, inner and outer. New friendships developed, and friendships recently made deepened.

I feel so lucky that I am here at Crosslands, lucky to have many friends, good friends both here and in other places. I had a very rich life with my husband for fifty years and with our children. Now my children are all leading busy and constructive lives. I have had an exciting and full life, and now things here are quieter and there is less activity, as is right for this era of my life. There is enough happening to be interesting, but not too much. I have pleasant goals ahead. My most imminent goal now is to spend February in North Carolina.

Yes, the year behind me is pleasant to ruminate on, and the year before me has plenty to look forward to in it. All in all, I have a lot to be thankful for. The year's end is a good time to ponder what we have learned from the last year, what challenges we met staunchly, what ones we did not do so well with. Perhaps we shall do better with our challenges in the next year. I wonder. What have I learned this past year? What do I want more of, what do I want less of? The year's end poses many questions. Some you can answer, some you cannot.

Thinking backward to the high points of the past year, I realize how many there were: planting my garden at Crosslands in the early spring, and the good feeling of the sun on my back and the earth in my hands; my visit to my two sons and their families in California in May; sitting on the sandy beach in Connecticut in August, smelling the salt air and listening to the small waves swish along the sand. How blue the water was, and the sky, and here and there a white sail passed. There was that phone call that told me my book had been sold and would be published; harvesting raspberries in the early fall, eating a few as I went along, and the luscious taste of the berries warm with the sun; the dazzling autumn colors we had; the good feel of the solid ground when the plane from Cape Cod to Boston landed after my recent rough and bouncy trip. I could go on and on. There was so much that was significant and very good during this past year, and a number of very high moments. Oh, yes, there were difficult times, too. Every year has its challenges, its low periods, its problems, its sad times. A year is some of everything, a beautiful mix, and through it all are woven the threads of growth. For we are always growing as a result of the happenings in our world, good and bad.

As I sit here beside my imminent crocuses, my poinsettia, and my azalea, I feel a wonderful sense of something completed, something finished. Yes, it has been a rich and rewarding year all told, the high points offsetting the low. And while I ruminate and hook, all these moments out of the past flashing before me are being worked into the rug pattern on my lap.

4 ❈

January Is Holding

And so the new year comes in—another new beginning to be stirred about. What will the shape of the year before us be? What happenings will mark the fresh page we have just turned? We can never look ahead and know; we have to just wait and see and be ready for new adventures in the offing.

There is a wonderful quote from a leaflet given out at St. George's Chapel at Windsor Castle:

> I said to the man who stood at the gate of the New Year, "Give me a light that I may tread safely into the unknown."
> And he replied, "Go out into the darkness and put your hand into the hand of God, that shall be to you better than a light and safer than a known way."

I have made two resolutions for the coming year. The first is to be more in the present and not dwell too much in the past or the future. Thinking back is not all bad. We draw strength from what has gone before. We gain self-confidence by remembering things we have done that worked out well. And as I have said, remembering can be creative. So looking back a bit is good and rewarding. Looking ahead can be a spur to action, especially when you have some intriguing goals. Planning for interesting events is stimulating.

For the most part, however, we want to be in the present, dwelling in the now. The past is really over with; the future isn't real until it becomes the present. So where we want our own main interests to be is in this moment we are living. This is really all we have.

Occasionally, the past or future captures your mind and you go about in a little bit of a haze. I know I tend to do this at times. Now, I am resolving to be where I am with all of my interest and enthusiasm, to be thoroughly in the now, to be alert and alive to exactly what is going on this moment in my life and to give it my all. I am going to work on this during the upcoming year.

My second resolution is to think more positively about everything. This doesn't mean to refuse to see a negative situation when you get into one, but to bring some positive thought or action to it. We are all faced with negative occurrences from time to time. If you face the facts and then think positively about them and engage in some constructive action about what you see before you, things work out better on the whole. Taking positive *action* instead of *reacting* negatively is a good rule, and one I will try to follow. These are both very *noble resolves!* Will I be able to follow through on them? That is the all-important question.

Sometimes in a group gathering someone will start criticizing the government, the way Crosslands is run, the play they have just seen, or anything. Instead of being lured into this negative swirl, I will try to bring some constructive thoughts to bear and lead the discussion around to a positive angle. I wonder if I can do this. Instead of absorbing the negatives surrounding me, I wonder if I can't give out some positive vibrations. I find that, for the most part, I am happier when I am thinking positively; I believe everyone is. So this is my second resolution for the new year ahead.

I also have a number of simple resolves, such as entertaining more, walking every day (this I do anyhow, but it is easy to get out of the habit), swimming regularly.

But I will really work on my two main resolves. Thinking positively, among other things, keeps you from fearing the future. Emmet Fox has said, "The road ahead may be veiled from sight, but you must teach yourself to regard the unknown as friendly."

Being in the now keeps you very much alive and alert. Douglas V.

Steere says, "Not then but now, not there but here is the Christian witness to be made."

As Abraham Heschel says, which I once jotted down in my quotes file from a magazine: "It takes three things to attain a sense of significant living: God, a soul and a moment. And the three are always here. Just to be is a blessing; just to live is holy."

With these thoughts from men whom I admire, I start the new year.

Snow is swirling up the valley, outlining the trees and their branches. The temperature is eight degrees. It is gray and raw and cold outside and comfortable in my apartment. Jane came over, and we were just crazy enough to bundle up and take a walk around the circle, my mile. Our fingers and toes grew icy cold, and my face was so cold I could hardly talk. We walked fast and didn't talk much and met no one; only a car or two passed. The snow gathered on our coats and woolen hats and blew into our faces, because there was a strong wind. The best thing about going out in weather like this is that it is such a joy to come in again. How warm and welcome my apartment was. And all the plants were glowing in their cheerful greenness after the white world outside. It was delightful to come in to my pink poinsettia and my red azalea. My first purple crocus is out and it is charming. My living room was warm and inviting. After a short visit, Jane left, hoping she wouldn't slither too much on the way back to her apartment in Kennett Square.

Tomorrow, I lead the Spiritual Growth Group on the subject of love. I have been studying Erich Fromm's *The Art of Loving* and making a list of questions to ask the group. It seems to me you could discuss love forever. It should be a stimulating afternoon. I hope I can do a creditable job. There are about twenty in the group, and nine have volunteered to lead, so we won't, any one of us, lead too often. I always have cold feet a day or two before I lead a group. Can I keep the compulsive talkers from disturbing things? Can I keep people on the subject? Can I keep them from bringing in extraneous experiences? Can I keep a feeling of love in the group while we discuss? Can I maintain a sense of the Divine Presence in our midst as the true leader of the group? I've been going over my notes a great many times. They will be a help. Will there be a good group? Will lots of the members come? This new gathering grew out of Francis Hall's seminar in November. It is our first meeting. I have a lovely prayer of St. Francis to read at the end.

> Lord, make me an instrument of your peace. Where there is hatred, let me sow love; where there is injury, pardon; where there is doubt, faith; where there is despair, hope; where there is darkness, light; where there is sadness, joy.

I just took down my Christmas decorations, including the pine branches. The little tin Mexican tree and the fat candles go in the desk drawer to wait there until next year. Christmas is over now and we are into the new year. It really brings an end to the holiday season and the old year to tuck away the decorations, which see the light of day but once during the year. And now I bring out my two Lalique birds from France, my carved, wooden woodcock, and my chunk of Norwegian glass with two wild deer etched on it. These items reside on the top of the desk. I haven't much room for such things in my small living room, so the desk top is a choice place for them. You do get attached to certain pieces of decor in your home, and these four items I dearly love. All were gifts from good friends at various times, and I've had them for a number of years.

Well, I can heave a big sigh of relief because the group meeting occurred today, and I think it went very well. There were ten there, a good size for a discussion. It was a wonderful group. Everyone was so articulate. I needn't have worried. They had plenty to say, they stayed on the subject, and there were no compulsive talkers. When the meeting started we were ten separate individuals. When it ended we were a group. It was fascinating to feel the transformation and be a part of it.

In the meeting we discussed whether or not you could bring love to a situation or relationship where it wasn't before; we decided you could. Is love something you can learn, or does it just happen? The general opinion in the group was you can learn it, and I believe this, too. Ardis Whitman says, "Love is not a single act but a climate in which we live, a lifetime venture in which we are always learning, discovering, growing. It is not destroyed by a single failure, or won by a single caress. Love is a climate—a climate of the heart."

I feel love is an art, something you can work with. Erich Fromm says some of the basic elements of love are caring, responsibility, respect, and knowledge. And he says having respect for a person means having an active concern that that person should grow and unfold as he is.

Sometimes we are very surprised that a friend with whom we agree on many points should not agree on some one other particular point, too. But we have to accept and, even more, appreciate the differences that occur and let our love bypass them.

Love, says Erich Fromm, is basically a giving, not a receiving; and in giving love we bring something to life in the other person. "This which is brought to life," he says, "reflects back. . . ." He goes on to say that "in truly giving a person cannot help receiving that which is given back to him. Giving implies to make the other person a giver also, and they both share in the joy they have brought to life."

I think this is a beautiful concept of love. In rereading Fromm's *The Art of Loving*, I am enjoying it all over again. There are many new concepts of love in it and much to ponder.

These are the days for indoors. Outside the ground is white with snow. The wind blows little drifts here and there. There is an interesting pattern of snow on the roofs of the buildings. Every building has a different pattern. The wind freezes your face when you walk, creeps down your neck, up your sleeves, and your ankles and knees feel the chill. No mile for me. I went over for mail, and that is as far as I am going today.

This is the day to ruminate back to last summer and remember the garden in its prime—the peas, how good they were; the raspberries, how delicious; the chrysanthemums, how beautiful *they* were; and the gold autumn leaves. I take out pleasant summer memories and, as if I turn them about in my hand, revel in the pleasure they bring.

We have to live in the now, especially with my New Year's resolution. Still, looking back brings moments of joy. While I polish furniture I indulge myself and relive the best moments of the summer and fall. Polishing furniture is my January occupation. Once a year I do this, and it is really a pleasure, also good exercise. Some of my furniture is very old and has been in the family for a long, long time; it is a joy to see the surfaces acquire a luster again. I am very fond of these pieces and find delight in working over them. I have a cleaning woman who comes once a week, but I polish the furniture myself because I like to. I enjoy thinking about all the various people the different pieces have lived with, all the homes they have been in.

Outdoors does not lure me. When I went over to post some letters a while ago and get my mail, my face nearly froze; so now I am in until dinner tonight. I will polish more furniture this afternoon and hook my rug. I am getting on well with my rug of the season. I do one every winter. This one is for my apartment. I've no room for more after that, so future rugs will be for the family. I want to keep on doing one a year. It is interesting to see the pattern form as I work and pleasant to hook when the weather is cold and uninviting.

While I hook these days, I think about next month in Tryon and my friends down there. I lived there for ten years and made some wonderful friends.

How much old friends mean to you. How I will enjoy seeing mine in Tryon. We have shared much—many experiences, good and bad. We have come to accept each other as we are. It is so relaxing to be with old friends. You no longer want them to be different. You want them just as they are. You know what to expect with them. I like what Thoreau said about friendship:

> Even the utmost good will and harmony and practical kindness are not sufficient for friendship, for friends do not live in harmony merely, as some say, but in melody. We do not wish for a friend to feed and clothe our bodies (neighbors are kind enough for that), but to do the like office to our spirits.

Thoreau also said: "I value and trust those who love and praise my aspiration rather than my performance. If you would not stop to look at me, but look whither I am looking and farther, then my education could not dispense with your company."

There is a time in our lives to go forward and a time to pause— just to hold. January is the month for holding, just holding where you are. I don't like to merely wait for time to pass; but during this month this is how I feel. A biologist once told me that experiments have shown that for the first ten days of January all of nature goes into a pause and there is no growth in root or top. Perhaps I am more related to nature this month than I think, because I feel as if I have been in a state of pause so far this year. I seem to have no incentive for action. I have to push myself to get going and to do the simplest things. It is certainly the time for me to hold where I am.

It is so cold and windy—every day the temperature is way down to zero, or six, or eight degrees. The sun is pale yellow these days, not the rich gold of summer and fall. It is more an idea than a warmth. The rhododendron hasn't uncurled in days. The roads are clear, but the ground everywhere is covered with snow. Even if you are full of ambition you can't make plans with any certainty, that is, plans to go anywhere, because we keep having more snow every few days. I believe the message from this month is: When things are difficult, hold where you are and wait. Don't get down and discouraged, but just go along evenly. Accept nature's pause for yourself, too. The sap and life of the plants are all deep down in the ground. This is the season when we, too, turn inward for our growth. It is the time for meditation, contemplation, reading, and thinking deeply about the world and our part in it, our pattern of living, our friends, everything.

I am glad I am not an Eskimo! I simply don't like winter, but we are in the middle of it and there are many weeks ahead of cold and snow, and I must get something constructive out of it. It's a beautiful time to sew and hook my rug and do needlepoint and visit nearby friends and have company for lunch and dinner. I dart out between snows and get something special to cook, and then I come home and ask someone on the spur of the moment to come for dinner or lunch.

Elizabeth Vining came over for lunch today, and we had persimmon and cottage cheese salad, nice hot herb tea, and baked custard. She is such a joy to talk with. We settled in the living room after lunch and discussed many things. Since Elizabeth is always writing, too, we talked about books and writing, and then I told her about the group meeting we had on love, and we talked about that for a while.

Great excitement! I just went to water the African violet leaves that I had potted in October and discovered that two of them have brand new tiny leaves coming up in the pot a little distance from the main leaf stem. The new leaves are very small and round and bright green. They have just pushed up through the soil. I've been watching carefully, and they weren't there a couple of days ago when I last watered; but they are now. And what a wonderful feeling this gives me! A wonderful feeling of the responsiveness of these violets. Now I shall watch carefully for the others to sprout, too. Out of ten, two have sprouted. One of the others rotted, and I cut it off and put the leaf stem down into the soil right up to the leaf itself. I wonder if it will take hold and grow.

This is the first time I have tried to grow African violets from leaves, and I am much excited to see it work with two so far. And now I expect the others to send up green leaves promptly. I shall be watching.

Something happens once in a while that gives you a very good feeling about human nature. Today was one of those days for me. The temperature has been zero or five below or some such every morning lately. We certainly are getting a dose of winter. My car has been very good about starting these cold mornings. As usual, it started promptly today, and I went to Kennett Square to do some errands. I made three stops and turned the engine off each time. The third stop was at the Acme. After shopping there, I settled my groceries in the back, and, alas, the car wouldn't start. It turned over, but didn't catch and go. I went back inside and called the Buick garage. The service man told me to press the accelerator to the floor and keep it there, and then if the car didn't start to call him back. I was trying this unsuccessfully when a very pleasant young man came along.

"I hate to see you having trouble starting your car," he said. "May I try it for you?"

I was delighted by his cheerful and helpful manner, and I slid over on the seat to make room. He seemed to do just what I had been doing, but with a special knowhow.

"You've got water in your gas," he said confidently as he worked with the starter. Finally, he got it going. I thanked him profusely. I thought it wonderful that he went out of his way to help a stranger, and so successfully. I like to think there are people like this around.

I drove to the Buick place, but they were so backed up with stalled cars that they said they couldn't work on it immediately.

I went and got a sandwich. There was another woman there whose car was also stalled. While we waited in the showroom we got to talking. Her husband had just died, so I felt a real sympathy for her. We talked a bit about adjusting to living alone. Finally her car was fixed, and then mine. No water in the gas, they said, but the carburetor and choke needed adjusting for the cold weather.

I got home in the middle of the afternoon. I had a good feeling all the rest of the day and evening about the kindness of an unknown man. The experience left me realizing again that most people are innately good.

Today was one of those days when you need to make something of yourself. It was cold, about ten degrees, and gray and snowing fitfully. Some days are made by the weather when you waken. This day was not. This was a day to take the message of January and hold.

It was the weather for indoor projects. I hooked my rug for a while, then ventured forth for a walk. I haven't missed many days in several weeks. Sally asked me to her apartment for a lunch of oyster stew. We had a beautiful meal together. I never ate such good stew.

She had driven in the new snow up to the White Barn Fish Market for oysters, earning my great respect. I simply don't drive in this weather. We sat and talked a bit after lunch. Then, I walked over to Katherine's to learn how to do the pine-tree pattern in needlepoint. She is an expert and a fine teacher. I really believe I can do it myself now. I'm making some eyeglass cases for friends, and it is a charming pattern.

Life is serene, quiet, with lots of time to contemplate these days and plenty of time for handiwork. I have three projects going at once now: needlepoint, my hooked rug, and neckties. Between all three, I can make these frigid days productive. Also, I cook dinner occasionally for friends. I've had dinner at home the last two nights for myself and one friend. Last night Jane and I had shad and fresh spinach and white yams, something I never ate before, never even heard of before today. Del Pino's Market in West Chester is one of our favorite places, and they had them. White yams are heavenly, even more delicious than regular yams. We finished off our dinner with fresh pineapple. Then we sat in the living room and talked a while before Jane went home.

I felt so good today I made a necktie from start to finish for the husband of a friend of mine in Tryon. I love making neckties and make quite a lot of them for my sons and various friends. I will soon get out my suitcases and begin to pack for Tryon. I always start packing ten days or so ahead. Then I have to take out of my suitcases things to wear, and sometimes I forget to put them back. So I arrive at my destination lacking a few items. My husband always packed the night before he departed. For this reason he forgot to put in certain things. So we always came out even—both with just a few things forgotten, but most everything important with us.

Last night it snowed. As far as you can see in any direction there is snow. Uninterrupted expanses of new snow are quite lovely. Nature and I have a rather distant relationship these last few weeks since winter came, but I have to concede that the new snow is quite beautiful, especially this minute as I sit in my apartment all cozy and warm and look out the double glass doors to the patio and beyond. The late-afternoon sun shining through the trees is casting long, blue shadows. Such interesting shapes they make on the whiteness. The evergreens in my garden are snow-covered and form smooth white mounds. Across the valley the bare treetops catch the sun and glow, while down in the valley itself all is snow and more snow.

A vast stretch of new-fallen snow is rather like the beginning of the new year. It is pristine and unmarked. What tracks will there be in a few hours, a few days? What shapes and patterns will form on the snow? What shapes and patterns will form in our days and weeks as we get more and more into the new year?

I took a walk today. It was cold and windy and the snow was blowing in all directions. It was invigorating but, as usual, I welcomed my warm apartment afterward. And I have been sewing all afternoon finishing up my second necktie for Tryon.

My daughter, Joan, came for the weekend, and what a gala time we had! She arrived at my apartment, having come from Boston by air at nine o'clock Friday night. I had dinner ready, a celebration dinner with lamb chops and white yams again. I also had fresh spinach, salad, and custard. We were eating dinner so late! But no matter—it was a gay occasion. I hadn't seen her since Thanksgiving on Cape Cod, and we had so much to catch up on.

We had a wonderful day yesterday with walks, a delicious swim, a visit to some of my friends, and lots and lots of conversation and exchanging of ideas.

This morning Joan and I went to Longwood Gardens. How refreshing to sit by the path in the conservatory where there was a bank of hundreds of paper-white narcissus and jonquils all at the peak of their bloom. Their fragrance wafted our way and we just sat there a while breathing it all in. Dozens of red tulips were also blooming. The sun was streaming in through the glass roof, and we were surrounded by the essence of springtime. It was a wonderful day outside, too. We are having a January thaw. How welcome after all that bitter cold. I've begun to consider what the weather will be when we start for Tryon in a week minus a day. We leave next Saturday, and it is Sunday now. I am nearly all packed—as far as I can go this far in advance.

Jane drove Joan and me to the airport about noon, and Joan was off back to her home in Boston. What a wonderful two days we had. We don't see each other terribly often, so each meeting is very special. With close family, you always begin just where you left off.

Jane and I set forth for Tryon, North Carolina, on Saturday morning, the last day of January. It was brilliant and sunny and cold. We had the car all packed. We'd spent some time yesterday settling things in the trunk and back seat: suitcases, coats, hiking boots, the double boiler (I never travel anywhere where I am going to cook without the double boiler), and the down quilt (I never travel anywhere in winter where I am going to sleep without my quilt. I like exactly one down quilt more than anyone else). We also had sandwiches for lunch; chicken, potato salad, and cooked peas, all in a little zipped cooler for dinner; and hard-boiled eggs for breakfast. We always like to make do without restaurants when we travel by car.

At every stop for gas it seemed to grow warmer. In a few hours the landscape changed to pines on both sides of the road as we went through Virginia. There was a little snow here and there, but not much.

A Ramada Inn along the highway welcomed us for the night. There we ate all our food except two sandwiches for tomorrow's lunch and two hard-boiled eggs for breakfast. We had our picnic dinner in our room and went to bed early.

5 ✿

February Is Not to Hurry

Sunday morning it was cloudy. We went so far on the previous day we figured we had only three and a half hours to go to reach Tryon. We could get there by noon easily. But life had more in store for us that morning than we counted on. At eleven we had one hour more to go when it began to rain, or was it snow, or was it sleet? It was all three at once. Finally it settled down to an icy rain that froze on the windshield in spite of our busy defroster. We slowed down. Everyone on the highway slowed, but even so here and there was a car off in a ditch, and here three cars had skidded and all were on the road at crazy angles. We just managed to pass. Along came a tow truck, and a police car, and an ambulance heading for the tangle of cars. On all sides of us cars were stuck. Almost all the bridges we went under had accidents on top of them.

We went slower and slower. Every car, including ours, had a layer of ice on the outside. We kept telling each other that maybe it was a little better here than a few miles back.

We stopped for gas, and my knees shook as I tried to stand. We were quite scared and wondered if we should hole up in some motel for the night; but we were in the wilds and there was no motel any-where. So we went on. Jane did nobly. She kept her head and reas-sured me after every downgrade that she hadn't skid when she gingerly applied the brakes. Then there came the time when she said she could feel the car skid as she braked. We looked around wildly for a motel. None in sight. Sometimes you find yourself in a bad sit-

uation that there is no way out of, only a way through. This is where
we were. We kept on going for what seemed like miles and hours.

All of a sudden we were aware that we hadn't passed an accident
in a few miles. It must be turning to rain, we thought. On the next
downgrade Jane said we were not skidding a bit. Still, we went about
twenty miles an hour. Something inside me kept saying, "Don't
panic, keep calm, and know that you both have been taken care of so
far, you both will be on to your journey's end." I wasn't too con-
vincing. But mile passed mile, and eventually the Tryon signs appeared.

Soon we went down the incline into Tryon, and there was the
A & P store, open on Sundays as always. Such relief we both felt!
We got out of the car, still shaky, and went in with our shopping
list divided.

"Can we say we made it yet?" Jane asked. "Not quite yet, I guess,"
she added.

It was a vast relief in the A & P to be thinking of earthy things
like butter and milk and bananas and lamb chops, and to have our
feet on solid ground.

Back again to our ice-encased car, and in we piled with groceries.
A few more ups and downs and plenty of steep curves and we drew
up in front of our house, a welcome port in a storm.

We turned to each other with great sighs of relief.

"*Now* we can say we made it," Jane said exultantly.

James came out to greet us. He is the very capable and pleasant
caretaker of the house. He looked solid and substantial and depend-
able after our adventures. He had to escort us individually up the
solid-ice steps. Inside the house was a roaring fire and his new wife to
welcome us. Nothing ever looked more wonderful than that familiar,
attractive living room and the crackling fire. James began unpacking
the car for us while we warmed ourselves and talked to his wife.

It was two o'clock. In our fright, we had forgotten lunch. After
James and Doretta left, we sat down to eat our sandwiches by the
fire. There were all our belongings piled in a corner of the living
room, and here we were at the beginning of our month in Tryon.

Jane would stay a few days. I would stay the month. She would return at the end of the time for the drive back.

All the while we ate lunch we were thanking heaven that we had arrived safely. The floor felt so solid and substantial. The house was wonderfully warm, and we were relieved and happy.

Every time I have come back here since my move to Crosslands I have started a new love affair with Tryon. This is the place where no one hurries. There seems to be all the time in the world for everything. I wander around Cowan's Market in a leisurely manner. I brought my knives down to be sharpened by Mr. Walker in the meat department. I leave them and amble over to the vegetable section. I meet friends from other years, and we stop and talk a bit. The sales people are friendly, remembering me, and when I leave, the checkout girl says, "Hurry back and see us now!"

A teenager wheels my packages out to the car and settles them in the trunk. I have a lot because I am buying staples. I am parked near a hydrant. Tryon's charms include the hydrants on the main street in town. They are painted like British soldiers, with red jackets, black helmets, and faces.

I am staying just about a mile from the center of town, and it is a pretty drive home. Anywhere you drive around here is beautiful. English ivy grows up the trees along the roadsides, festooning the bare branches with greenery. Great rhododendron bushes grow there too, and whenever the road is on a north slope there is bright green moss at the edge of the pavement and on the roadside banks.

January jasmine is blooming, the gold starry flowers tumbling over bare branches. The woods are full of tall, straight pines and oak trees with their crisp brown leaves still clinging, waiting for the new spring growth to push them off. Everywhere you look you see a silhouette of mountains through the trees. Tryon is surrounded by the foothills of the Blue Ridge Mountains. They change colors through the day. When the sun first rises early in the morning, Hogback Mountain looks reddish from my window. Then, as the sun rises higher, it turns gold. Through the day the mountains are blue, and at dusk they turn slightly violet. I stop for gas, and even such a utilitarian process is a pleasant interlude. At the Gulf station, the man there remembers me and greets me by name. We discuss Tryon and Pennsylvania and the weather in both places while the gas flows into my car and he cleans the windshield.

I drive home to Whispering Pines, the name of my house, with my shopping bags of groceries, and I am well contented. I had company last night for dinner and will have company tonight, and I will go out to the Tea House on Lake Lanier for dinner tomorrow. My erstwhile friends are so welcoming and cordial. It will be a sociable month, and I shall love it.

I really enjoy cooking, and I love my little house. The kitchen is a delight and full of sunlight all day long. The living room has windows on three sides and mountain views out every one. From the bedroom I see mountains, too. Every morning James comes and lays a fire and brings the paper and mail. I light the fire in the late afternoon and keep it going through the evening. By the time I go to bed it is just red coals bedded in ashes. After I am in bed there is the familiar sound that I love—the distant whistle of a passing train.

February is not to hurry. This is the message of the month for me.

After we crossed the border from Virginia into North Carolina on our way down from Pennsylvania and before it got icy, we stopped for gas. The gas attendant was a wonderful, aged character wearing an old, battered, felt hat on the back of his head. He looked a bit battered all over and entirely unconcerned about it. He ambled forward to us with a friendly "How you all?"

He looked as if nothing could ever hurry him, and then I remembered what I had forgotten since my visit last year—that few people ever hurry here. We got our gas and left, being invited to "hurry back," which was amusing, considering the complete lack of haste everywhere.

And then I begin remembering the leisurely ways of the South and of Tryon in particular. I go into the market to shop and find myself engaged in conversation with the vegetable woman. Oh yes, I have a list and I want some apples and what would be the best cooking ones? "Rome apples for cooking," she assures me. I want to make apple ambrosia for company in a few days. I have company two nights in a row, and I make enough dessert for both the first night.

When I go into the drugstore to buy postcards, I find myself discussing the different cards and the views with the sales clerk. And I get into a long conversation in the Blue Ridge Weavers about what you could use Fines Herbes for (I was buying a bottle of them). It is just a different approach to living, and I love it. I slow myself up about one hundred percent and flow with the people around me, and this fills me with a feeling of basic relaxation.

Every afternoon I sleep an hour or more—every morning I walk a mile or more or swim.

Why do I hurry in Pennsylvania? I don't have to. In spite of my resolve when I moved to Crosslands, I do hurry at times. Actually, I don't too much, but other people do. Many people there are brisk and rushed and very, very busy. This becomes sort of contagious, and sometimes I find myself catching by osmosis the feel of rushing.

If you hurry through a woods walk, for example, you don't see the wild ginger leaves just beginning to come up, or the glorious ancient stumps of dead trees, probably chestnuts. If you hurry through a morning, a day, a week, what a lot you miss! This will be a leisurely month, and I will take my leisurely feelings home with me to Pennsylvania, where I shall adopt the southern tempo and try not to let go of it.

Life is lovely to savor, and when you move in haste through your day you don't have time to ruminate as you go and to savor, and all you have at the end of the day is a lot of surface impressions. When you ruminate or contemplate or savor your day, you are nourishing the spirit. Being uncertain of just how to nourish the spirit, we attempt to stifle its demands and needs in a madness of outer activity.

So the message I get from February is not to hurry, to slow down and savor.

There is an old Chinese saying that I am very fond of: "Hurry slowly, and you soon arrive."

I have been thinking about the simple ways of living and the more sophisticated ways. Both have their place.

In our sophistication we find our true dimension. It draws us away from the simple things, or tends to. In the degree to which we can recognize this, and from the midst of our sophistication hold to the basics and to things less complex, our true dimension is revealed to us.

It is raining—my mountains are obscured by mist. The stone walk to the door and the brick terrace are wet. The laurel and the holly leaves in the woods are shiny wet. The clock on the mantel ticks in a businesslike manner, and it chimes the hours. A fire in the grate is blazing, bringing a lovely fragrance to the room. I have two wood baskets of logs to burn today. I always have a fire in the evenings, and on a day like this I have one all day too. A fire is friendly and sociable. You are never totally alone when you have a fire. But there is something wonderful about being here with my fire and my clock, with my needlepoint at hand. Since this house is at the end of the road, no one passes by. Here I am in a state of solitude. Solitude in winter by the fire is as rewarding as solitude on my terrace at home in October. Solitude anywhere at any time of year is a delicious state in which things come up from our depths. It is a part of inward renewal. If there is no silence, words lose their importance. There is a need for us to listen—to others, to nature, to our own depths, and to God. If we do not listen, speech has no meaning.

Without some solitude in our days, our activities become meaningless gestures. There needs to be a careful balance between silence and speaking, between solitude and participating in events. This balance forms the underpinnings of graceful and gracious living.

As I sat by my fire, I began to think about growing older and its advantages. A kind of gracious easiness descends upon you. No longer are you in keen competition in any area of your living. No longer do you feel the need to rush about so much. You find yourself just naturally more interested in being than in doing.

You begin to know you can't change other people. You may, if you work at it, change yourself, but you aren't likely to effect any real changes in another person.

You know now that you probably won't set the world aflame or change it very much.

You have learned that other people very seldom want advice. They want and need to be listened to with love and caring, but not to be told what to do.

You have learned that, as has been said, "A friend is someone who leaves you with your freedom intact." And you have become this kind of friend.

All this adds up to a gracious easiness that descends upon you; and you revel in it.

My house here is in the Thermal Belt. The mysterious Thermal Belt is all through Tryon in various places. There are warm winds that come up from the plains and drift up different valleys and mountain draws and make certain areas in the vicinity warmer than places a few hundred feet farther up the mountain or down. Sometimes when you look across at the range of mountains that shelters Tryon you can see a line of frost above and below a space where there is no frost at all. This is the Thermal Belt. Some people will have ice on their bird baths one morning while a neighbor up the mountain will have none.

My outdoor thermometer registers seven or eight degrees warmer than the official weather station in town. It's cozy, wrapped round by the Thermal Belt. I like it. On a sunny afternoon recently the temperature was seventy here and sixty-two downtown.

I just balanced my checkbook. This makes me feel very good. You see, I can't always balance it, so when I do it is cause for a great celebration and a feeling of jubilance.

My mother lived into her nineties, and to the day she died she always played bridge, which she loved. Her mind was sharp and keen to the end, and she always said it was because she played bridge. Maybe so—probably so!

I don't play bridge, but I keep a budget of everything I spend and I balance my checkbook. I work at making both come out right. I often wonder if these two activities equal bridge and if my mind will be good to the end. Well, I am sure I don't know, but I hope so.

At any rate, my evening is made tonight because the checkbook came out perfect the first try. Sometimes I have to struggle and do it over several times. If I give up, then I take it in to Myrtle at the bank in Kennett Square, and she works on it and gets it to balance and points out my mistakes to me. I feel my bank is especially amiable to do this for me.

Back here in Tryon where Bob and I lived so happily, I think about him and I realize I live in two worlds—in memory, a world with Bob, and in actual living, a world without him. When we grow older we lead two lives, the past and the present. Sometimes the past seems more alive than the present, and here it returns, sometimes in waves. This is good and bad: bad if you remember with sadness and longing, good if you remember constructively with a sense of gratitude that you had those rich moments. You can actually remember creatively by letting the backward glimpse give you joy and add enrichment to the present. It has been said that there are two kinds of people, creative people and noncreative people. However, I feel that everyone is creative in some area of his or her life. And I *know* that there is such a thing as creative memory. The word *creative* is much broader in scope than it might appear at first glance.

What a perfect day! It began when I woke to streaming sunlight and a temperature of nearly fifty. First I went swimming with Eleanor. She picked me up, and we drove to the swim-club pool. It is large and lovely, fifty feet by thirty. We were the only ones there, and the water was smooth and unruffled. There is nothing more re-laxing than swimming, than being buoyed up by the water and watching the sparkles formed by streaks of sunlight that shine through the glass roof. There are countless rainbows and moving pat-terns made by the sunlight on the water. To swim through this gives me a sense of being in some enchanted spot. There seems a touch of magic all around me. I don't know any other pool where you can swim back and forth and look out the glass side at a whole line of mountains. The trees are bare, and through them the range is sil-houetted against a very blue sky. This morning the mountains seem as if they had a wash of lavender over them. And they are so clear.

This afternoon I went for a walk with Betty. We went down past a stand of bamboo. The bamboo here is lovely in winter, with its firm, smooth stalks and bright green leaves. The breeze blew through it, rustling delightfully. We were in the woods, and the leaves under-foot were ankle deep and crunched as we walked. They sent up a very special smell. We came upon the heart-shaped ginger leaves and the leaves of the cane fly orchid with their interesting purple undersides. The leaves of this flower last into the winter, then die, and the orchid without foliage blooms in early summer. Betty knows all the plants of the woods here and points them out to me. We are following trails this morning, and I am thinking of a quote that I like. I don't know who said it. "Do not follow where the path may lead, go in-stead where there is no path, and leave a trail."

I am having such a great time here with my old friends. Every day I spend time with one or another of them. I have had dinner com-pany or gone out nearly every night. It is fun cooking for my friends and going to their houses. This is a heavenly month. It is flying by.

Tonight I will talk to Joan on the phone. We converse every Sun-day. This is something I treat myself to, and always have since Bob died. It makes me feel so close to her. She shares her week with me and I share mine with her.

This has been a happy day, and a happy day leaves a lovely echo through the year.

When I go walking in Tryon I come across enchanted bits of woodland—so lovely they are difficult to describe. Perhaps these two haiku I recently found will do it for me.

Above tides of leaves
That drown the earth
A mountain stands
Aloft, alone
                    Buson

A river leaping
Tumbling over rocks
Roars on
As the mountain smiles.
                    Meisetsu

Everywhere there are mountains and there are streams. The mountains are very near, not way off on the distant horizon; some days they are so clear and appear so near at hand you feel you can reach out and touch them—almost. Bob always told me never to walk in the woods here alone, so I never do. I go with Betty. She knows the area so well. She always has a plan when we go, and I rely on her. She is capable of going far longer than I, but she kindly adapts to my speed and distance.

Jane telephoned me today to tell me all the news from home. Also that she had planted peas in my garden at Crosslands! It's the earliest I've ever had peas planted. They are having a streak of warm weather there, and she couldn't resist a little gardening. And that was the most likely thing she could do. Will they really grow, survive some frost, and actually bear peas? I wonder, and I guess that was how she felt.

Just a few more days. Three, to be exact, before Jane and I head for home. It has been a superb month. So heart-warming seeing and being with old friends. It has been beautiful here in the mountains with the weather warm and perfect. Jane arrives in a few minutes. Eleanor met her at the airport.

This has been not only a fun month, a beautiful change, a sociable time, but also a little nudge in the direction of remembering not to hurry through my days, my weeks, my life. The message of February, of the South, is always not to hurry.

6 ❀

March Is to Be Aware

What a good feeling when, at noon, we turned the car in at the Crosslands gate. Then another good feeling opening my apartment door. The first thing I did after a quick look around at all my familiar things was to go over to the African violets. The parent plants were fine, and more of the little rooted leaves that I had potted in October had sprouted. Six out of nine had flourishing little plantlets in the pots. Only one had died. This was an exciting moment.

Now this evening everything is unpacked, and I am sitting in the living room appreciating, just appreciating what is around me. Furnishings create a mood. And I like the mood my things create. I have missed this mood, and now I settle into it comfortably.

I love possessions! Perhaps this makes me some dreadful kind of materialist. Nonetheless, I love possessions. There is the old desk—a family heirloom. It has cubbyholes and a front that opens down. I keep the brass drawer handles on this desk bright with an annual polishing in winter, and the desk itself, too. The apartment has that nice, clean smell of Johnson's floor wax when I finish rubbing the maple wood of the desk. On one side is a curved mark, slightly indented. Bob told me the desk was being moved once from one house to another as an inheritance. It was in a horse-drawn cart and it swayed over the side, rubbing against the wheel. I envision that moving day long ago whenever I polish this favorite piece of furniture and rub wax into that curved mark.

Then there is my maple bed. It was one of a pair of twin beds Bob and I bought when we had been married just a few months. The posts at the four corners have a carved pineapple design. Recently, a furniture refinisher was looking at this in preparation for some work he was going to do on it.

"A nice antique you have there," he said.

"We bought it when we were first married," I replied.

"Yes, it really is a fine antique," he repeated, running his hand appreciatively up one of the posts and over the headboard.

This put me in my age group neatly.

On my wall is a picture of three gaily colored ox carts on a street in Costa Rica and a view down the street to mountains. It was painted by a Costa Rican artist we once knew and was in her exhibition in New York City many years ago. Bob and I loved it on sight. Some friends engaged to be married were with us at the exhibition. We all admired this picture. They occupied our little house on Cape Cod for their honeymoon, and shortly afterward an express truck delivered us the picture, carefully crated. It was their thank-you for the cottage. I love the picture more every year I live with it.

A cuckoo clock is a sociable affair. Mine is one of my favorite things. A good many years ago I went to visit my sister in Cincinnati, and one day we found ourselves in the German section of town. The next thing I knew I had bought a cuckoo clock, quite a large one, not pausing to consider how I would carry it on the plane. It had beautiful dark wood, long chains and weights, and of course a little door at the top where the bird came out and cuckooed. Somehow I coped on the plane, and Bob, who was used to my bringing things home on planes and remembered the great kite I brought one time from Haiti, took it in stride. We hung the clock in our living room. I moved it wherever we moved. I still have it, and it is very important to me.

On our first trip to the little mountain village of St. Luc in Switzerland, Bob and I stayed in a hotel that backed up to a woods. I remember waking the first morning there and, in my semiconscious state, I heard a cuckoo and found myself counting to see what time it was. I got beyond twelve when I realized I was not at home and it was a real cuckoo, the first one I had ever heard!

Whenever I am away I am always glad to get home to my cuckoo clock. And to all my possessions.

I suspect everyone has cherished treasures from years back: old silver that feels good to handle, plates that are a treat to use, furniture you love to live with. Are we all materialists? Perhaps not. Anne Morrow Lindbergh has written that beautiful possessions are physical expressions of spiritual values you believe in.

I had a stack of mail waiting when I returned from Tryon, and gradually I went through it. I picked up a large envelope. In it was a copy of the jacket of my new book, *The Touch of the Earth*. It is charming: a white background with a light blue columbine flower, and my name in light blue. And now my editor gives me the news that she will have copies on March 27.

It's a fine thing to go traveling and an equally fine thing to come home. I am enjoying just being here. As I looked out the window today at my purple and gold crocuses in bloom and the view of my valley, as I look around my apartment now, and as I think of my special friends whom I will be seeing very soon, I realize that *home* is a wonderful word with a wonderful meaning.

Appreciating my apartment and thinking about the rewarding month behind me, I am aware that the month has told me things, too, things I needed to know. I loved being in Tryon for a month, but I realized that I didn't belong there as a resident, just as a visitor. I really belong in Crosslands. This is no longer my era for living in Tryon.

These last three years at Crosslands I have pined a little for Tryon. I have said my heart belongs to Tryon, and one little corner did, but my head tells me I belong in Crosslands. Now I feel, although I love Tryon and always will, and love to go back to visit, and have nostalgic moments even thinking about it, my heart and head unite in telling me I belong in Crosslands. Being the age I am, being alone, there is no longer any question. The people here are my people. This place is my place.

And when I go to bed tonight, because it is a starry evening, I will drift off to a sleep looking out the window at my tree with twinkling stars tangled through its bare branches.

Kay telephoned me from the Cape to say that Del had been taken to the hospital in the middle of the night with a heart attack and was very, very ill. She was terribly upset and crying on the phone. This is frightening. He had a heart attack a year ago.

I woke up to a white, white world. It started snowing in the night, and now every branch and twig is white. The sky is white, the air is white, and snowflakes are sweeping up the valley in drifts. On the bushes around the terrace mounds of snow weigh down the branches. It is an enchanted world this morning. My crocuses are out of sight under a blanket of white.

All day it snowed hard. The roads became impassable. The men were out shoveling the paths, and the plows were on the roads.

But March snow has an air of impermanence about it. The ground is warm. It won't last. While it is snowing, the terrace is wet and melting at the edge of the snow. But before the snow stopped we had nine inches.

It was slushy for a day or two, and then the snow was gone.

The very first beginnings of spring are here today. The wild geese are back. Every day a new flock flies overhead, and some geese drop away from the flock to settle on our pond. Are they considering nesting this early?

Everywhere over the countryside the large willow trees toss their streaming branches to and fro. The exciting thing is that these branches are now gold—a part of spring's beginning.

Then there are my African violet leaves that are sprouting. Isn't this, too, a sign of spring? The little leaves are so tiny, bright spring yellow-green, and filled with promise. Norma, my next-door neighbor, took good care of my plants when I was in North Carolina.

Outside on my patio, under the window where it is protected, my first crocuses are in bloom: purple, lavender, white, and one yellow one. In other parts of the terrace garden are more crocuses here and there in small clumps and clusters. This is the time of year when crocuses are my favorite flower—perhaps because they are the first. It is cold, thirty-two degrees in the morning, but still the crocuses open up by noon. And the sun shines down, gilding the bushes, bare trees, and evergreens all around. It is not the white sun of January now, but a very gold one. The light has a different quality, too. There is a softness as it shines down on the gardens everywhere. The buds on the maples are swelling, and the buds on the forsythia look imminent.

This is one of the most stirring beginnings of all, the beginning of spring.

What is the message of March? The message I receive from the month of March is to be more aware, more observant, more alert. So much is happening every hour; if we aren't careful, we will miss a lot. To begin with, every hour there are new signs of spring, and we don't want to miss any of them. The grass has hints of green through it. Did it have these yesterday? I don't believe so. Yesterday the wild geese were flying in flocks; today here and there you see pairs separate from the groups. The hearts of my chrysanthemums were yellow-green with beginning leaves when I uncovered them a few days ago. Happily, I found them all alive. They are a rich, deep green now, a few days later. The sun on the back of my hand and my face is really warm all of a sudden this morning.

Listening is something that is also a part of being aware, and really listening to your friend while you are together is a special kind of awareness. If you really listen you hear more than the words expressed; you hear beyond words to the state of being of your friend. If she does the same for you, you really relate to each other in a new and deeper way.

So if you increase your awareness, you will be catching the early signs of spring and many messages from nature that reveal the basic rhythm of the earth. But also, you will find yourself becoming more aware inwardly of people's attitudes and feelings in groups and separately, and this enhances all your relationships and your very being.

I have been thinking about spiritual stature recently and how to judge it in ourselves and in others. It seems to me that a person's spiritual stature or lack of it is revealed by the size of the things at which he takes offense.

Whenever anyone does something or says something that upsets me, I pause and remember this, and it brings me up short some times. How very healthy!

I call Kay every day or so, and the news on Del isn't good. She is terribly upset. Should I go there and be with her? Maybe so. I will see. She would like me to come.

I am sitting out on my terrace surrounded by early spring. I have been pruning the prostrate juniper and the clematis, which already have buds all up and down the stalks. The temperature is fifty degrees; everywhere birds are singing. There is a little song sparrow that perches on my birch tree as he warbles his melody to me. Down in the valley the sun glints on the water of the stream. I took the plastic covers off my terrace chairs and settled in one in the sun. It is great to have the season of sitting out come again.

It is fine to realize that winter is over. Or is it? That is the thing about March. One day it is winter, and the next day spring. First it is sunny and warm, and the next day a blizzard descends. This is the most unpredictable month of the year.

Lilja Rogers wrote a charming poem about March in an old issue of *Saturday Evening Post*, that I saved in my quotes file.

> First a howling blizzard woke us
> Then the rain came down to soak us

And now before the eye can focus—
Crocus.

It was raining in a misty sort of way when I woke up. After lunch, in one hour we had four different kinds of weather. First, the mistiness turned to hard rain for a few minutes, then it turned to hailstones, and presently the ground was white with them. Soon, a brilliant sun appeared and shone down dazzlingly for about twenty minutes, melting the hail. After that, a real twenty-minute blizzard descended. This tapered off into a misty rain again, which is what it is doing now. March is a wild, restless month with a cold wind a lot of days and many sudden changes. I am sewing on the terrace in the morning, and by afternoon I am snug inside while the wind howls outside. You need to be adaptable to conditions in March. In all living we need to be able to adapt to sudden happenings and accept what comes.

It is cold and sunny with a strong and chilly March wind. This is the month the whole landscape has a scrubbed clean-swept look. The maple trees' red buds are expanding, the forsythia buds are swelling, and crocuses bring their gay colors to the small terrace gardens here. Today is a momentous day—the official first day of spring. Jane came over this morning and we planted peas. She dug up the ground and I planted them in a trench with cow manure. I sowed the seed very thickly. I never follow the directions of one to two inches from seed to seed, but scatter them much closer. And they flourish. The ground is just barely thawed, with still a few frozen clods of earth. It didn't take very long to do our gardening. The sun shone down on us; the wind blew us about; the earth was cold to touch. It was a good feeling to be working in the soil again, but we were glad to come indoors afterward.

I plant according to the moon. Crops that mature above the ground go in when the moon is waxing; those that mature below the ground go in when the moon is waning. And you don't go near

the garden for four days in the dark of the moon. The moon is waxing now, so it is right for sowing peas.

There is no sign of the peas Jane planted in February. We dug
down discreetly in one spot and found a sprouted seed. So we
haven't given up. But it is over a month ago that she sowed the seed.

Today it is fifty degrees outside my door and there is brilliant sun.
I went down into the vegetable garden this morning and planted
spinach and parsley. How great it was to be handling the earth. It
was soft and moist today, and my little planted rows looked filled
with promise when I finished. I put up chicken wire for the peas to
climb on also. My first gardening day when it was a delight to be
out! No one else was down there. I was alone. No sign of rabbits or
coons or deer or pheasant or any other wildlife. It was quiet. The
sound of the stream flowing by was all that I heard. And suddenly
some wild geese flew overhead in a small and dignified V, just nine
of them all together. The bare tree branches on the hillside facing me
were gray. The fields looked bare and swept clean. No visible sign of
growth anywhere. But there was a feel of growth in the air, a feeling
of things happening underground, the sap flowing up into the limbs
and branches, and just a slight hint of a pink cast over all the trees,
suggestive of buds to come. It was still and windless in the garden, as
if all nature was holding her breath before the uprush of life, so imminent.

There is a kind of weight on my spirits these days about Del. He
seems to get worse, not better. Kay has a housekeeper with her, so
she is not alone. I write her every day or so.

Del died today. I called Kay tonight and heard the sad news. I
couldn't go to sleep for a long time. I kept thinking about Del, how
wonderful he was, and how I would miss him. And then I began to
realize how momentous this was for him to be making the great
transition to the next life. He never believed in the next life. He felt

what we have here is all there is. We used to laugh about it, and I would tell him how surprised he would be when he died to realize he wasn't dead at all.

He said he certainly would be surprised, and that it was complete nonsense about an afterlife. What we had here was the beginning and end, and that was that, so there.

You either believe in life after death or you don't. You can't prove it one way or another. You just feel it. I more than feel it. I know it as a positive fact, though I can't say why exactly. Life here on earth proves it to me. There couldn't be just this much and no more. I feel this world and our life here is a learning, growing experience. The next life is perhaps more learning of a different kind. I know with everything in me that when I die I will be with Bob, and it will be some kind of a new beginning. Dying, I believe, is a great transition, but never an end.

Sir Rabindranath Tagore writes, "Death is not extinguishing the light but turning out the lamp because the dawn has come."

For Del, the dawn has come.

Without a sense of the immortality of our souls, this life would lack meaning, purpose, and intelligence. There just has to be a life beyond this one. I sincerely believe in it. I like to think Del is in it now, and knowing that it exists, how surprised he will be.

In connection with the afterlife, there is much emphasis on light. Mark Van Doren wrote a lovely poem about it in his book *That Shining Place.*

How far is it now?
When will there be
No more, no more
Of time or of me?

No telling, I know
And so I should stop
Wondering how soon
The great weight will drop.

And darkness be all—
Or will there be light
More of it, more of it
Blinding my sight

As meteor swift
As butterfly slow
Down the deep universe
Dazzled I go?
—"No More, No More"

I see immortality as a gift of heaven, as a result of the incarnation of God, the living Spirit, in man.

I love to think there is another life after this one. What a great adventure this makes of dying! What an experience it will be! It seems reasonable and right that what happens to us in the next life relates to the logical outcome of the use we have made of our lives here.

I believe that when our bodies are no longer fit for the soul, the soul and body separate and the soul leaves, taking the individual's personality with it. I see this life as a gateway to a broader life. Del is now having this great experience.

Today was a real spring day, warm and sunny; but just to remind you it is still March, there was a chilly wind around the edges.

Jane and I drove to the two-hundred-year-old town of Marshalton, about a half hour off. Our purpose was to see the famed three acres of winter aconite and snowdrops surrounding an old homestead. It seems that two hundred years ago a man named John Marshal (for whom the town was later named) built his home there. He happened to like winter aconite and snowdrops. Instead of a lawn under the great trees on his property, he planted these by the hundreds, in drifts and masses. The results today are so lovely they attract visitors from all over. In the early spring there is always a car or two parked on the road outside the old stone wall that surrounds the place. The present owner is very proud of his display of flowers, I have been told, and welcomes those who come to look and admire.

I walked up the road toward the old homestead to get a view from another angle. I met a stern-looking elderly man walking down the road.

"I feel I am trespassing," I said apologetically. "Your flowers are so beautiful I wanted to see them closer, so I came up here."

"That's all right," he said rather gruffly, "as long as you don't dig them up."

"Oh, I wouldn't think of that!" I exclaimed, horrified. "Would anyone?"

"You'd be surprised how many people come here and start digging up these flowers to take home," he said, thawing a bit.

"They're so beautiful," I said, and we went on talking a few minutes. He seemed more and more human and pleasant and even began to smile. He liked my appreciation. I have found everyone likes to have his garden admired.

"Say," he said finally, "why don't you dig up some and take them home? Wouldn't you like to? You may if you want to."

It had been interesting to watch his metamorphosis!

I thanked him, but said no, we must go along. I went back to the car where Jane was waiting.

After several more minutes of admiring the flowers, we went to the Marshalton Inn and had a delicious lunch. The old inn is as ancient as the town and still has a few hitching posts for horses out front. After lunch we drove home feeling slight waves of spring fever. There were hints of green in the fields we passed and swelling buds on all the bare-branched trees along the roadside.

My crocuses in the terrace garden are just beautiful and more numerous every day: purple, lavender, yellow, blue, and white. I have scilla out, too, and one hyacinth shows a blossom coming up out of the center of a cluster of bright green leaves. The chrysanthemums have green foliage in the heart of each plant, and the forsythia shows hints of gold along the bare branches. The rhododendron has large, fat, promising buds. I love all these first signs of spring.

I was sitting out on the terrace reading this afternoon when Jane stopped by. We went down to Heritage Gardens and got some lawn fertilizer and some butter crunch and Great Lakes lettuce seedlings. Half the sky was blue and sunny, half black and ominous. Showers came and went as we drove along. How great to buy our first young plants. The lettuces were so green and firm and perky. Now they are on my terrace, bringing spring to my area.

Heritage Gardens was beautiful. The greenhouses were filled with bloom: pansies, primroses, African violets, daffodils, azaleas, and countless other flowers. How welcome all that color was after the muted tones of the landscape.

Two more of my African violet leaves have sprouted, making eight out of nine growing.

This is the last day of March. The temperature is seventy degrees. Birds are singing everywhere. The forsythia is in full bloom, both mine and Frank and Emily's next door, creating a great wave of gold. The wind has died, the air is soft, and the sun is warm on my face and hands. The grass is really green. The rainy day we had yesterday brought out the color. The buds on my weeping birch are green-tipped and the catkins greening. The landscape is changing almost as I watch. I feel spring emerging around me. As I sit here quietly on the terrace in the sun, I am aware of furious activity going on in the earth. I can almost feel the uprush of life in all the trees and in the soil everywhere. I hear the distant call of wild geese over the hill and a crow or two. And now a plane flies by very high in the very blue sky—just to remind us that civilization is still right there, too, and that we live in two worlds, the natural world and man's world. We have one foot in each.

This is the season we emerge from man's world of houses and in-doors to nature's world. But we need always to be in both worlds, with an awareness of both—the world of people and feelings and emotions and things, and the world of outdoors, of growth, and of a Force greater than us! It is our ability to blend these two worlds within us that matter and keep us in balance.

7 ✿

April Is Living This Moment

It is a beautiful experience to participate in the change of seasons. And one of the most exciting to be a part of is winter to spring. The change goes on quietly for several weeks, quietly and gradually. There are hints of the new season to come every day. But the season that is passing clings a little. Winter clings a little through March with a chill wind and an icy day and maybe some snow; but then there are warm days, too, and a warming sun. Perhaps we are somewhat like the seasons in the way we so often tend to cling to the past, the familiar, and hesitate before something new and untried.

Every day new things are happening outdoors and happening fast. The willows that were tossing their golden branches about in March now have green streamers of tiny young leaves. There is a brush of green along the roadsides and in the woods as new leaves begin to unfold. Almost all the trees have buds swelling and visible. You sense spring hidden in their branches and twigs waiting to burst out into leaves. Some already have a green cast over them. When you drive about you get an occasional whiff of fresh onion grass. You also hear the first peepers in the marshy hollows, while daffodils all over are blooming and magnolias and weeping cherries are beginning to flower.

All through the area are splashes of yellow forsythia, like fountains of gold. Everywhere the birds are singing; from the car you occasionally hear a strange and unfamiliar bird, and you wonder. The grass is greener every day. The change has been gradual and graceful but now is really here, and I am loving it. My daily walks are a joy. The pool is reconditioned and painted, and those of us who like to swim have started going over again.

I am spending long hours on the terrace reading, writing letters, or just appreciating spring and listening to the mating call of the pheasants down in my valley and to the birds all around. I am always fascinated by the world of birds and wildlife that interpenetrates our own world. To be aware of these other worlds makes our lives richer and more understanding. In a small way we can be a part of these other worlds as we increase our awareness of them.

April days are glorious, and they join us all to something basic and lasting and eternal.

Lately, I have been having dinner company one night a week. I like to cook and entertain. Shad is in season, and fresh asparagus and fresh spinach are all so good these days. That is my menu recently and, of course, dessert, one of my favorites. I have a great file of dessert recipes. I extend myself in this area for company.

I woke to a cloudy Sunday morning. I was eating noon dinner with Carol and Faith at the Center when all of a sudden we noticed it was raining hard. How fine to have the rain we need. We especially enjoyed our meal to the accompaniment of the shower. We haven't had nearly enough rain this winter or spring, so every shower is a blessing. When I returned to my apartment I stood looking out on the terrace watching the rain descend. I could almost imagine I saw the tiny beginning leaves of my weeping birch unfold as I watched. Then along came a cardinal and perched overhead on a branch of the cherry tree in the rain, and I realized those leaves were coming out also. He gave his rich, mellow call, and somewhere his mate answered. He called several times, and each time there was a response; the response grew nearer and nearer until they both were in the cherry tree. What beauty they brought to my outdoors—the gold of the forsythia in a wave below them, along with Norma's brick-red tulips, my hyacinths and blue scilla and chionodoxa, and the very green grass everywhere.

The crocuses are gone for the season now, and in their stead are my daffodils full out. Next fall I am going to plant a hundred more daffodils. That is the thing about gardens: You stand among your plants in the present, and ideas for the future drift into your mind. I must have more daffodils, even if I have to look at all the tops in the tall grass for a few weeks. You can't cut them until they die back. I'll just put up with that because daffodils are lovely in flower and very much a part of spring.

This afternoon at about four o'clock Jane came over and said it was the moment to take a walk. I took a sort of dim view of walking in the rain, but she was all set with a raincoat and umbrella, so I got out mine and off we went. I was so glad I did, for it was just beautiful to be out in such a greening world. Each tree and bush we passed had beginning leaves. And we were in a world of forsythia. There is a great deal of it around Crosslands. Everywhere the rain darkened the tree trunks and branches, put a shine on the road, and made a delightful sound on our umbrellas. You could almost feel the earth respond. I've been feeling especially happy ever since it started to rain today.

Now it is suppertime. I have my terrace door open and can hear the melody of a thrush down in my valley and the sound of a pair of wild geese flying overhead. And while I look at the hillside of trees across the valley, I realize that just this afternoon they have become touched with color as the buds develop.

At this moment there is even spring in my apartment. On the dining table are seven stems of deep blue scilla in a tiny vase I brought from Greece.

What message has the month of April for us?

As I listen to April and get the feel of the month, I find I am being told to live in the moment. This is the message I receive. It is the month to emphasize and reiterate this one of my New Year's resolutions: to live today and enjoy each hour as it comes all day long. Obviously, we all have to make some plans and have goals ahead and arrange for them, and this we do; but it only takes part of the day. Then we can take each moment of the rest of the day as it comes and live it to the fullest, enjoy it, be thoroughly present in the now! April is a special month for this because every hour things are different outdoors. If we are with it every moment we are outside, we see so much more and become a part of nature's changing pageant of springtime.

If we live in the now, we get a real feel of the people we are with. We get a true sense of situations, and we relate to our friend or friends on a deeper level. Living in the now, you enjoy everything much more. When in a group, it is easy sometimes to let your mind slip away to some private concern, and then you have a faraway feeling and you aren't truly there with those you are physically with. You lose your perception and your awareness and you miss what is going on.

So this is the month to be where we are in the present moment—feeling it, sensing it in all its varying shades of meaning, all its tints and tones and aspects. When we live in the moment, we are living with awareness in mind and spirit. We are fully alive, maybe in a quiet and unexpressed way, maybe in a quiet and expressed way. When we live in the moment, we are flowing with the stream of the world.

I bought six broccoli plants at Heritage Gardens and planted them in my vegetable garden. They looked so healthy and flourishing when they were all in and watered, with wire put around them to deter the rabbits.

There is a waxing moon, so the time is right. They should do well. It seems that moon rays are as important as sun rays in the healthy growth of garden produce. If you plant at the correct phase of the moon, it will be full and shine on the young plants at the time of their growth that does them the most good.

My peas are up, the ones Jane planted in February and the ones I planted in March; also beets and spinach. The plants are tiny but there. I planted more peas so I hope I will have a succession of them in June. I do like fresh peas from the garden.

I just drove into town to the florist and ordered an arrangement of spring flowers to be sent to Joan next week. She has to go to the hospital for surgery and a stay of about a week. A very nice young woman at the florist's telephoned Boston and told the flower store there to make it a special bouquet because it was from the young woman's mother. It will arrive the day Joan has surgery. The surgery isn't a serious matter, but it is something that must be done. I am a little concerned and will be glad when it is over and Joan can put it behind her.

I woke up this morning to a day of brilliant sunshine and to the delightful realization that here was a gift, a whole day with no plan, no commitment, no date, no must or ought to—a whole day to do with as I chose.

Jane and I decided that we would celebrate spring. What better way to spend this heavenly day. Wherever you looked there were blossoms, a soft blue sky, hints of spring greenery, and the spirit of spring itself was in each of us.

We set forth with light hearts. We left my terrace area with forsythia and daffodils glowing, tulips tall and straight and very red, scilla very blue, everything else burgeoning, and little furry catkins swinging on all the branch tips of the weeping birch.

We drove first to nearby Longwood Gardens. The entrance area was truly lovely, with sweeps of snowy white flowering crab apple and pink cherry trees. It was fairyland. We left the car and started to walk—first over where there are great stretches of daffodils naturalized under and around magnolia trees in full flower. There were star magnolias and the regular saucer varieties. A sweet fragrance drifted through the air, and we were just about overwhelmed by the loveliness of it all. We walked slowly through the very green grass surrounding the area, taking everything in. There must have been thousands of daffodils and dozens of magnolias.

From here we wandered through an area of pines, cool and dimly lit and delightfully fragrant, and on to a path toward the conservatories. On the way we came across some Norway maples with their exotic flowers in full bloom.

A very wise person recently told me about the strength we get from trees, living near them, walking under them, being around them. I believe this. He also said we should stand for a few minutes sometime with our backs against the trunk of a tall, straight tree and our hands at our sides; some of the tree's strength will flow into us. We each chose a Norway maple. They were large and firm and stately. The bark felt rough against our backs, but not unpleasant. In fact, it was a very agreeable sensation to stand against a large tree, just stand there quietly taking deep breaths. There was no one in the garden to decide we were crazy, so we merely stood there a while, peaceful and happy.

Then we walked over to the conservatories, and they were sensational. One house was filled with azaleas and cymbidium orchids and had a stream down the middle. The next building was aglow with fragrant Easter lilies and delphinium like none I had ever seen before—about eight feet tall with huge blossoms that were light blue, dark blue, purple, and white. Tulips were everywhere, as were hyacinths. We were truly overcome by everything and sat down to take it all in for a while. There was a cart of potted hyacinths nearby, ready to be set out. Jane and I each borrowed a pot, courtesy of Longwood, and held it as we sat there. We were looking at delphinium and breathing in that delicious fragrance of our private hyacinth. Several people passed by, each asking where we had bought the hyacinths. When we explained, they were much amused. So were we. It was a delightful few minutes.

Jane and I don't always talk when we are together. A companionable quiet springs up between us. It is an especially rich friendship when this happens, when two people sense each other's warmth and don't need to talk about it.

After a bit we put the hyacinths back in the cart and wandered into the orchid house. I always love to go there and smell the beautiful scent of white cattleyas. It reminds me of the very happy years when Bob and I lived in Connecticut and had a small greenhouse off the living room filled with orchid plants.

Jane and I went on to the rain forest where dripping roots trail down all over the place and banana trees grow. This reminds me of the Guatemalan rain forests where the ferns are ten feet tall.

After we left Longwood we drove out into the country on some back roads, passing weeping cherries and magnolias; everywhere there were splashes of gold forsythia. At one point we came across a bank of daffodils beside an abandoned house. There were no inhabited houses anywhere about. We stopped and picked a large bouquet of these small, gold, trumpet flowers to take home. While we were picking them, we got a sudden spring shower. How fresh and wonderful was the scent of the earth in the rain as we gathered the flowers. Picking flowers along the roadsides is one of my favorite pastimes. There is something slightly illegal about it that I enjoy and that lends zest to the occasion.

The countryside was beautiful. We saw many farms with large, fine white barns and hex marks. Several had silos with metal roofs that glinted in the sun, which had just come out again after the rain. Here and there was an Amish horse and buggy, and often we saw horses plowing the fields. Everywhere were cows and horses, green fields of alfalfa, stone walls, and fences with tumbling honeysuckle in bud.

We thought it would be pleasant to get lost, so we turned off the familiar routes down a back road. We went to the right and left as the spirit moved us. Soon we were completely lost, and it was delightful. All along the roadsides was shad bush in bloom, and once we came to a bank of bloodroot in full flower. We slowed up to appreciate these, while a little breeze ruffled their petals. They are such dainty flowers and so pure white. They are called bloodroot because if you bruise the root the juice is red.

When we returned from celebrating spring it was late. With all the beauties of nature we had seen, we had almost forgotten lunch. This was a morning to remember.

I slept soundly after lunch for a while and then went over for a swim. The pool is beautiful, newly painted. The water is very blue. The plants around the edge bring a note of nature indoors, and the sun sends shadows over the surface ripples and sparkles down deep. After my swim I went to see Edith, who lives in the intermediate-care section. She has bad arthritis and doesn't get around much. I was telling her about my day, my day that started out with no plan and just unfolded hour by hour into one wonderful experience.

Sometimes our best days are those that start out with no specific plan but in which you follow the urges of your spirit through the hours. Now tonight I am writing here in bed, thoroughly content, relaxed, and ready for sleep.

It is raining hard, drops of water are bouncing on the flagstone terrace, and mist is blowing up the valley. I hear the sound of the rain against my bedroom windows. It is a fine day to accomplish things in the house, but I can't seem to get anything done because a bouquet of daffodils I recently picked is on the dining table. I have to keep stopping to look at them or smell them. They are so beautiful. Each one is different. One is pure white, trumpet and all. One is white and single, with a frilled pink center. One is white with an orange center, another yellow with a deep orange frilled center.

I like to look at them where they grow at the edge of my bank, but sometimes I have to pick a few for indoors so that I may see them close up and smell them, and then I feel spring in essence.

A friend brought me a large armful of peach blossoms yesterday. I have them in a tall bamboo vase, and they are sensational. They are fully out and deep valentine pink, and they greatly enhance the room.

Perhaps one of the exciting aspects of this glorious season is that it doesn't last very long. First thing you know, summer is here and the delicacy of spring colors and the spirit of spring is past. I won't think of that now, but just enjoy this beloved season to the full while we are in it.

This was a week of music. Two days ago there was a beautiful concert at Crosslands by a cello group from the New School of Music in Philadelphia. We had music by Bach, Villa-Lobos, and Menotti. The musicians were young people and completely charming.

Yesterday I went to the Academy of Music in Philadelphia to hear the symphony orchestra. It was an enchanted afternoon. Klaus Tennestedt conducted. A twenty-four-year-old genius, Shlomo Mintz, who started playing the violin at the tender age of two, performed Prokofiev's Concerto no. 1 magnificently.

The last number was Dvorak's Symphony no. 8. I don't believe I had ever heard it before, and I was quite carried away by it. I rode home in the bus in a totally dreamy mood. I felt the mood of the music all evening.

It is Good Friday. Six years ago today my husband died—after fifty years of a completely wonderful marriage. My daughter said, "It is only given to special people to go on Good Friday, and father was a very special person."

Two and a half years later I moved here to Crosslands. For all these six years I have been in a state of transition, undergoing a kind of inward and outward upheaval. It has been a difficult period, perhaps the most difficult of my life. Making the adjustment to life in a community wasn't easy. But making the adjustment to life lived alone was of course the part that was the hardest.

I have one firm conviction that has helped me through a number of crises in my life, and it helps me now. I believe that everything that happens has a reason, a purpose. We don't always know what that reason is, but I believe it is there all the same. This helps me to accept what comes. Now and then I wonder what the reason is that Bob died at that time and that I am living life alone now. We were very close, and I depended on him a lot. Can it be that I needed to learn to be more self-sufficient and independent? I wonder. It has worked out that way. There are probably more reasons than that. And I think they all have something to do with the development of my soul. That is what we are here on earth for, isn't it? That is the purpose of this life, according to my convictions, and all that happens contributes to this end.

Once, a few months after Bob's death, I felt that I no longer wanted to live, that life held nothing more for me. But then I began to realize that everything happens for a reason, that I needed to be alone for some reason. This conviction helped me past the crisis.

Now, six years later, I have not only firmed up the conviction, but also developed a degree of acceptance of Bob's death and all that is related to it. I don't feel I have to know reasons; I just accept that they exist. And I know that it isn't my time to go yet. I have more to learn here on earth.

I have in these six years learned to get along with loneliness. I have always liked a degree of solitude, but that is different. That is pleasant. Aloneness is unpleasant. I don't believe I will ever stop missing Bob. But I have, in a sense, made friends with the state of my missing him. I have procedures—things I do when I reach that mood. A wise friend once told me that, when you get in a bad mental state of reaction to some situation, the best way out is to act instead of react. That is what I try to do. It isn't always easy, and sometimes I fail and have a low few hours, but most of the time I can work my way out through a variety of activities: baking bread, asking someone over for a meal and getting involved in cooking it, working in the garden, telephoning someone long distance, cleaning out cupboards and closets—any forward-going action that will help lift me out of these missing moments.

Just recently something rather wonderful has been happening. I find I have a sense of Bob being with me quite often, almost any time I think of him. I feel his nearness, I sense his presence and his guidance if I have decisions to make. I have the comfortable feeling as I sit here in the evenings alone that he is with me, that I am not alone. I feel him with me when I am in the garden, especially, and when I listen to our favorite records, when I enjoy something beautiful—a sunset, a moon rise, a starry night, a symphony, the feel of spring.

I feel I have made great progress in these six years, although I am sure I have farther to go. Haven't we all?

Looking across my valley at the hillside of trees stirs my sense of wonder. It is such a soft and lovely sight. Each tree is a slightly different shade of golden green—spring's color. Some still have bare branches, and a few have a blur of red over them in the sun.

In my apartment is a potted white hyacinth I bought to celebrate Easter. My living room is full of the fragrance of this flower. It is on the dining table, and I eat breakfast and lunch with the hyacinth scent.

All is well with Joan. I have been calling her each evening since her surgery. I am so relieved. The last time I phoned she sounded quite like herself. She loved the flowers I sent. She says she will be home for Easter.

Last night in the auditorium we had a moving hour of Easter music. There is a fine choral group here and several people who play instruments. Willard, a retired organist from a New York City church, trains and conducts concerts several times a year. He does a splendid job. This time we had some Bach, and Handel, and a couple of hymns we all joined in singing.

After the music was over the whole room was silent for several moments, still under the spell of it all, especially the last piece they sang, the spiritual "Were You There?"

What a wonderful day! The copies of my new book just came in the mail. It was terribly exciting to open the large package and glow a little. The autographing party is to be in a couple of weeks in the Sunflower Shop, the gift shop here at Crosslands. Will anyone come and buy a book? Will people like it? Will the reviews be good? All questions without answers yet.

What does Easter mean? There is the Bible story in all its beautiful symbolism, and that is thought-provoking. There is an inspiring feel of new beginnings and new life everywhere in nature. In these last weeks the trees have gone from bare and dead-looking branches to small, burgeoning, very-much-alive new leaves. The grass is transformed from dead brown to brilliant live green, and flowers are everywhere. In the fields in the area, wild mustard tosses its golden blooms in great sweeps and dandelion blossoms enhance the landscape.

At the Easter season new life seems to spring into being, not only in nature, but in us too.

There is a kind of added vitality that comes to us these days. This is the Easter of it. While the sap is rising in all the trees and bushes, we sense it as if the sap or something comparable is rising in us at the same time—some extra energy, a sense of added life, a kind of special joy. Maybe you find yourself humming a little tune as you set out small lettuce plants or scatter lettuce seeds down a straight furrow. You leave the garden for the house and you bring something special indoors with you that lasts several hours. You take this particular feeling with you over to the Center to have dinner. As you come home after dinner you see the lights in the buildings. They aren't merely lights in a building, but each one is a special home, a place of caring and interest. The first stars stir your sense of wonder. Is each another world? And can there be life on some of them?

For a brief instant you feel a particular at-one-ment with all the homes here and the people in them, with the neighborhood and the people you don't know, with our country, with the world, and with the whole great and mysterious universe and its myriad stars.

We can be grateful for Easter and this lift of our hearts and the feel of the flowing life force surrounding us and within us, and the promise in the very air. We take this in, with gratitude. We can't thank nature for these things; we only can be grateful, humbly grateful. But I feel we have an obligation to life to take what has entered us from the world around us at this Easter season and make something out of it; not to give it back to nature, which doesn't need it, but to pass it on in some form to another person or other people.

Perhaps we are most fully alive when we are conscious of the precious gift of life. Our consciousness of this is intermittent. It ebbs and flows. We don't maintain a continuous consciousness of this great gift. We get the sense of it in short glimpses here and there, now and then. The moments when we become aware of this great gift lift us out of the ordinary, give an added quality to our day, our week. For a little while we transcend everyday things. Our lives take on an extra dimension. We reach peaks in living, in awareness. And we have a keen sense that we are living in the now.

8✿

May Is Listening

ay comes in quietly in a sweep of snowy dogwood in full bloom; purple and white lilacs everywhere are sending their fragrance through the air. The wild mustard in the fields is even golder than last month, and along the borders of the roads the lavender red bud is full out. Now and then when driving about we get a whiff of wisteria. Is there any scent lovelier? Azaleas are dazzling in the gardens of Crosslands. The viburnum carlesii is so sweet to smell. And what dignity the tall tulips bring to the area as they open out in all colors.

Elizabeth took Helen and me on a picnic today—the first picnic of the season. We went north on Route 100 through fields newly ploughed and great and prosperous farms. Everywhere were flowers and flowering trees of all sorts. We passed a few orchards in full bloom, their fragrance wafting our way. All the towns and villages we drove through were burgeoning with spring blossoms. I never saw so many and such large lilac bushes. They sent their flowers up to the second story in some instances. Occasionally, the scent of newly cut grass would blow our way.

A few dark clouds developed and we had a sudden and brief shower about lunchtime, so we drew off the road. We settled under some trees and ate our lunch in the car to the sound of rain on the leaves. Surrounded by newly leafed-out foliage in beautiful shades of spring green, we seemed bathed in beauty and we surrendered wholly to it. All three of us have special feelings about outdoors in the spring and natural beauty.

We were in a hilly area as we started driving again after lunch. We passed little villages, remote and charming. Eventually we came to French Creek Park and explored that area. I had no idea where we were much of the time, but Elizabeth and Helen, being native to these parts, seemed right at home with all the remote side roads we were on.

When I got back I felt as if I had been miles away, and I was filled to the brim with beauty and spring. I reveled in the relaxed sleepy feeling that came over me, and I slept for an hour before dinner.

Such a gala day from start to finish!

It began with a beautiful, clear morning of sparkling sunlight— cold but lovely. This was the day of the luncheon to celebrate the publication of my book. Carol was our hostess. There were five of us: Carol, Sally E., Sally M., Virginia, and me. We drove to Wilmington and had lunch in the DuPont Hotel's Green Room. When we went in it was filled mostly with businessmen. After a bit they left, and we had the place to ourselves. It is a beautiful room, with heavy, dark, wood carving on walls and ceiling. I so seldom go into a hotel in this country I felt as if I were in Europe, where Bob and I had stayed in so many fine hotels. We ate in a leisurely manner. Several of us had eggs Benedict, which was marvelous. We ate and talked, exchanging ideas on various subjects until quite late, then drove home. The drive both ways was beautiful, with flowering trees all along the roadsides.

I ate dinner with Sally M. at the Center, and we came back to my apartment and sat and visited for the evening. I went to bed feeling my book was now happily launched, and it was a good feeling.

I love plant sales and nurseries in the spring!

And today I experienced both. The plant sale was at the London Grove Quaker Meeting House. The wide porch was gay with red geraniums, flowering alyssum, verbena, yellow marigolds, and dozens of other annuals, as well as healthy-looking delphinium and phlox and many perennials—a little of everything. People were filling cars with armloads of plants in little boxes, while everywhere around us the pink and white dogwood flowered. Sally and I left with armfuls of petunias, marigolds, ageratum, and alyssum for both our gardens.

Hockessin Nursery, one of the loveliest in the area, was another one of our stops this morning, and it is where I got some miniature zinnias.

First I planted the little marigolds. Each plant had one or two lemon-colored blossoms. They now border my terrace garden and look charming. I also planted the ageratum. I will set out the zinnias tomorrow.

Tonight my hands have an earthy look about them. I am so eager to get my hands into the soil the first part of the season that I never wear gloves. After a little I will wear my garden gloves, but at first the earth is so delicious on my bare hands that I have to experience it. Today I set out my little plants, watered them, cleaned off my trowel, and came in feeling a contented glow. While I was out there down on my hands and knees digging in the garden, it seemed to become part of me, and I became a part of it. Time ceased to exist. There was just the earth, the plants to go in, and me. We three.

Every year I say I will wait until the middle of May or later to set out small plants, but then in early, early May quite unexpectedly I find myself buying little plants and digging them into the garden. In spite of all resolutions, I succumb to spring and can't wait. Don't we all succumb to spring in one way or another?

What is the message of May to us?

The message I get from May is to listen—to listen more carefully in all areas of life. There is so much to listen to in nature these days: the sound of the wind rustling through young leaves, the songs of the birds, the quacking of the ducks in our pond (seven newly hatched ones), the scratching of a turquoise beetle on my flagstone patio floor as he rushes over to seize a passing ant and demolish it.

Nature is alive with sounds, and we hear them all with pleasure and delight these spring days.

Then there is listening to another person. So often we are filled with our own ideas demanding expression that we do more talking than listening. Occasionally, we are with a friend who has a problem and needs to be listened to. How much listening, really listening with love and caring, can help!

Douglas Steere says, "To listen another's soul into a condition of disclosure and discovery may be almost the greatest service that any human being ever performs for another." He goes on to to say, "Over the shoulder of the human listener... there is never absent the silent presence of the Eternal Listener, the living God."

The third kind of listening is listening to ourselves, to our intuition, to our deep center, to the spark of the Divine within—to God. We will be guided aright if we hear God speak to us in the silence and if we listen and heed.

So I will let this be the month of saying less and hearing more—listening more, in all areas of living.

I was wakened out of a sound sleep at five-thirty this morning by a bird flying against my windowpane over and over. In a slightly dazed and half-asleep state of mind, I could not figure out his motive or *his* state of mind, nor could I go back to sleep—he was very persistent. Birds, I reasoned as I lay there fuming silently, aren't supposed to have much brain, but they are reputed to have great instincts. What strange instinct was prompting this annoying little character to fight my window? Whatever it is, I decided, will have to stop, because I don't relish starting the day at five-thirty.

Now, I really like birds when they perch on tree branches or fly around the sky. When they keep to their normal routine they are a joy to watch and study. But this one must have been out of his mind. What would I do?

After consulting a few people I finally learned from Sally Coppes, who knows as much about birds as anyone here, that in the spring when birds are nesting each pair stakes out its own territory; the male fights off any intruders while the female sits on the eggs. This little song sparrow was fooled into thinking his reflection in the glass was an interloper. He was defending his area.

That was all very well for him, but what should I do? And why *my* windows instead of anyone else's? There are a whole row of apartments on this side of the building, all with identical windows. The ways of nature in general are mysterious and the ways of birds in particular, I find, are equally so.

Jane came up with some netting she had used to protect our blueberries from the birds in the garden last year. With heavy tape, some staples, and this netting, we covered my bedroom window in such a way that the bird could not reach the glass. This was a rather difficult procedure. It took balancing between the chrysanthemums in the garden below, the window, and the madonna lilies and teetering back and forth on my little kitchen stool.

However, what bliss to wake up at eight-thirty the next morning instead of five-thirty. There was the bird hopping up and down the netting; but he couldn't reach the glass, so all was silent! Problem solved. For me—but am I giving the bird a nervous breakdown?

Of course, I have to look out at my superb view through some ruffled netting!

If only I didn't have a bird finding enemies in my window pane.

There are always a goodly number of "if onlys" in each of our lives. As I have said often before, we need to be able to accept these "if onlys" and take them with equanimity to get along in life.

If only the rabbits hadn't eaten my lettuces. If only there weren't all those woodchucks, rabbits, and coons licking their chops and waiting for the garden to grow a little more so they can feast! If only it would rain hard for three days and really soak the earth.

I am sitting in my living room looking out the glass doors to the terrace. I see the dark, purplish-brown trunk and branches of my cherry tree through a lacy pattern of green as the young leaves blow in the wind. In my terrace garden each evergreen has yellow-green tips of new growth on every branch. The wind is blowing hard. The little weeping birch responds by streaming its leafy branches out toward the east. It is interesting to see how each tree and bush beside the apartments here take the wind differently. Some bend with it, flow with it; some resist it, buck it. Each has its own way, sort of the way we take the happenings in our lives. Each one of us takes them differently.

Across the valley the trees are a poem of loveliness, all in various shades of green. From where I sit I look into their tops and see patterns made by their shapes and the branches and trunks weaving through the greenery. The vision I have of this hillside seems not to be of this world. It is not related to the everydayness of our lives and the daily happenings. I like to sit in my practical living room and be transported to this ethereal world of nature—and then come back to the everyday world. How important both are to us! We need one foot in each world, and the spring of the year is the time when we slip readily from one to the other.

I talked to Kay tonight on the phone. She was feeling quite low. I know so well how difficult those first few months are when you begin to come out of the numbing shock of realizing that your husband has died. I worry about her because she has the added problem of not seeing well, so her activities are somewhat limited. And activities do help keep you in balance. I am glad that I am going up there the middle of this month for two weeks. Perhaps I can help her by just being there. Yes, I do worry about Kay these days.

I have decided something recently about worry. People sometimes react to concern by saying, "Forget it. Put your mind on something else." But I have discovered a better and different way of handling worry. Accept it, take it with you through your days, live with it, see it for what it is, make friends with it. If you push worry away, it intrudes again and again. You also miss the chance of growing a little. Every bit of concern and worry that you take with you and live with leaves you farther along the road than you were when it came. Pretty soon after you have faced and handled it, it drops behind of its own accord. You don't always think this to be true, but I have found it so, and a comfort to experience. So I am trying to make friends with my concern about Kay.

One and a third inches of rain fell yesterday afternoon! Cheers!

Such a heavenly, sunny spring morning!

I went down to the vegetable garden and found, alas, that the rabbits had eaten more tops off my young lettuce plants. They had burrowed under the fence. I was pretty mad; then I realized that it was merely the same "if only" I needed to make my peace with. These things just happen, and you can't get too hot and bothered about them. So I calmed myself down.

My garden is burgeoning otherwise. I settled there to cultivate the whole thing, all along my rows of peas, beets, spinach, parsley, and broccoli. How good it was to loosen the soil and thus demolish all the tiny weeds that were just springing up. And of course it looked beautiful as I worked along. I believe my lettuce will grow out again, even if partly eaten. There were several people down there working in their plots. I like community gardening. It is a good feeling to have companionship while you cultivate and dig, as the sun shines down on you all. The many plots are thriving and filled with promise as their owners work. I like everything about cultivating, even the scratchy sound of my tool in the soil. As I progressed, the earth and I seemed to develop a perfect understanding.

Pretty soon the others left their gardens and went on up the hill and I was by myself—but not really alone. Solitude is not necessarily aloneness. There I was in the garden loosening the soil, hilling up the rows. I was surrounded by birds singing in the trees along the walls, and the music of the brook flowing past, and the sound of a number of interesting beetles on the earth. I had for company all of nature. You are never alone in a garden.

Sometimes it takes will power to keep our days simple and free so that we have time to garden and to do other things that are important to us. Will power, however, cannot make vegetables and flowers grow. It is our care that causes a response in the garden. The seedlings we cultivate and water spring up and become productive plants and flowers that give us pleasure and joy.

Gardening and cooking have some things in common. You give your time, your caring and love, and the results are astonishingly beautiful—and, in cooking, delicious. But before you receive you give. The rewards of your gift of time and meticulous care are flowers, delectable vegetables, bread, cakes, cookies, and such.

Giving and receiving are closely related. First you give, and then you receive—in other areas of life, too.

When there is an orchid in the refrigerator there is usually excitement afoot. That is the way it was with me yesterday. It all began at Sally M.'s, where Jane and I went for a lunch of a special Chester County dish: creamed, chipped beef and mushrooms on waffles. Heavenly! This was a farewell party for Jane, who leaves in a few weeks for a retirement center in Lancaster about one hour from here. She has been living in Kennett Square. This luncheon started off my special day.

But it was for dinner last night that I first wore my orchid, a beautiful yellow cymbidium made into a corsage and given me by a dear friend. I felt very festive.

The autographing party began at six-thirty at the Sunflower Shop, the gift shop here at Crosslands. People came and went for an hour or so buying books, talking, looking at books. It was so gala and so much fun. It kept me busy thinking up different things to write in peoples' books. I was surprised that several people I didn't know at all, or at all well, bought books. You never can tell. Surprises and delights. All in all, quite a number were sold, and it was a very merry occasion with a truly good feeling of warmth and friendship all around. There is such a nice awareness of the fact that people here at Crosslands warmly support a fellow resident when he or she has moments of prominence. It gives you a very pleasant family feeling.

After the autographing party was over I went to Virginia and Willis's to a party to celebrate further. We had champagne and toasts and sat about and talked a while. This just put the finishing touches on a day of lovely experiences.

And then this morning I found myself out in the garden in sparkling sunlight watering my recently set out marigolds, ageratum, and zinnias. Such an interesting change of pace. I like both places.

All the fun wasn't over yet. My book's publication continued to be celebrated tonight when I was invited to the Old Mill for dinner, where I had delicious roast duck and there was a fabulous salad bar! When I got home I was wonderfully contented as I autographed and wrapped up books to mail to family and close friends. And now I am sleepy and so to bed feeling very peaceful and happy.

Mother's Day. I wore my orchid to church and to dinner at the Center and felt very festive. In the dining room they gave all the women orchids. So then I had two! I received a lovely Mother's Day card and letter and phone call from Tim and Jeanne in California. A call came from Joan in Boston. She has just accepted an offer of a job in California and will move out there the middle of June. I will certainly miss her, but the job with a computer company sounds ideal, with all sorts of opportunities and places it can lead. Instead of a weekly phone call, we will have to start a lovely correspondence. Joan is excited about her future, and so am I.

I did not get a call from Bob and Susan because they are off with friends for a boating holiday in the Caribbean.

A very happy Mother's Day altogether.

The little plane made the trip from Boston to Hyannis Airport successfully, with a minimum of bumps, on a clear and beautiful day, and I arrived on the Cape as planned. Kay and Mrs. Miller, her companion, met me.

Here in every dooryard garden are masses of tossing lilac blooms: white, lavender, and purple. The beach plum is out, too, and snowy white along the roadsides, and the gold of Scotch broom tumbles over banks here and there. Spring is at its beginnings and very lovely.

We walk, we go to see nearby friends and a niece and nephew who live here. But mostly we talk, sitting out on the lawn in the sun with the whole Atlantic Ocean before us and the waves breaking on the sand below our bluff. Sometimes we drive around in the car, and in the evenings we sit by the fire in the living room, and maybe I read aloud or we talk more. All the while Kay tells me how it was with Del his last few months and when he was in the hospital dying. I feel for her. I remember so well just how I felt after Bob died and what a relief it was to talk to someone who listened and understood. So I listen and try to understand.

What do you do and say when, on a beautiful, blue, sunny spring day, with all the world smiling, someone tells you she wants to die? This is a puzzle. I had my time of wanting to die, too, when Bob had been dead just a short time. So I know how Kay feels. But life is not planned so that we can die at wish or will. Wishing to die, therefore, is futile. We need to live until our time comes. The need is for us to make the best of what we have and do the best we can even when our hearts are heavy.

I told Kay that what had helped me when I was in that phase was to realize that everything that occurs in this life happens for a reason, and that there was a reason why I was alive and alone, and that it has something to do with our spiritual growth. Kay doesn't see things this way, but perhaps one day she will get hold of some other bits of philosophy that will help her. I hope so. Meanwhile, on this visit I can only listen to her and then share with her the things I believe and that have helped me. If she doesn't accept them, I can do no more.

Kay does not see the forty-five years of a wonderful marriage she had, but only the last difficult weeks. I guess I was the same. Probably we all are.

I am remembering the conversations with Del last November about eras. It is so hard for dear Kay to accept that one era has ended for her, that there is a need for her to accept and begin another one—another phase of life that will be quite different but will have its own very different joys and where she will find peace and contentment. I do not believe that we ever get over the loss of a beloved husband of many years. But we do make our peace with the situation. This is quite possible and largely how we weather it.

Kay is filled with sadness and regrets. All the things she wishes she had done differently before Del died haunt her. I remember being haunted by the same thoughts myself. I just hope I am being of some help, but sometimes I wonder. She is so filled with her own suffering that she really cannot hear what I say. I guess it is best if I just listen. This is how it is after two months of widowhood, I can well remember. I also recall that it was a help to have someone I was close to around; Kay and I are close, so maybe that aspect aids her. Sometimes I read aloud, or she dictates letters to me, since she doesn't see well enough to write them herself. And so the days slide by.

One evening we had a wonderful lobster dinner—fresh boiled lobster from the fish store in town. We had them cooked and cracked for us and brought them home hot, and then we dunked the delectable morsels in melted butter. It was an ambrosial meal.

Of course we miss Del. How he used to enjoy our lobster dinners! We always had them when I came up here for a visit.

And now we have a series of gray days with a silver sea and the waves breaking silvery white along the sand. Our walk today took us down a lane where apple blossom petals blew like snow along the road ahead of us. Then we stopped and ate our picnic lunch on the brink of the Mill Pond, watching the tide rush through the narrow inlet and the terns fly overhead.

We stopped at the little cottage Bob and I used to own. It was nearly hidden beneath masses of lilacs that I had planted many years ago. It was closed up, and we picked armsful of lilacs and carried them home. Tonight we sat in the living room by the fire smelling the lilacs while great gray gulls flew over the house, dipping down to the beach in front of the place.

Our conversation tonight was about children and grandchildren. Kay has three fine grandchildren. There are two themes that haunt Kay: the last week of Del's life and the three grandchildren she worries about. They are fine young people, teenagers and college age, products of divorced parents. But they beautifully survived the broken home. I wonder if her worries are justified. I wish I could help her, but my feelings about grandchildren and children are quite different than hers. I believe my philosophy about them developed after first reading Kahlil Gibran on the subject of children.

I feel we must let go of them when they are adults. When they suffer from their mistakes we suffer too, to be sure, but still we have to let them make their own mistakes. They do not belong to us any more, but to life, and they must be freed.

Kahlil Gibran writes in *The Prophet*:

> Your children are not your children.
> They are the sons and daughters of Life's longing
>   for itself,
> They come through you but not from you,
> And though they are with you yet they
>   belong not to you.
> You may give them your love but not your thoughts.
> For they have their own thoughts.
> You may house their bodies but not their souls,
> For their souls dwell in the house of tomorrow,
>   which you cannot visit, not even in your dreams.

9 ❀

June Is to Loose and Let Go

June is the beginning of summer. The leaves on the trees are fully out and lush and green. The grass and fields everywhere are green. It is a green world we live in now, with flowers all over the place. On the lawns at Crosslands are drifts of white clover blossoms. My valley is filled with great masses of tiny white wild roses with yellow centers. They are fragrant, and the scent wafts up to where I am sitting on the terrace. When we drive around we pass banks of honeysuckle in full flower and mounds of these same wild roses. The scent floats in the open car windows, honeysuckle and wild roses mingled. The air is warm and caressing. The sun shines down. June is a gentle month, and it begins with a gentle day.

In my terrace garden the white clematis is full out and lovely, especially in the moonlight. The purple jackmanii is also opening. The little marigolds and zinnias, set out before I went away, are flourishing. I water them and pull a few weeds while bright yellow goldfinches fly about in the wild cherry tree. Down in the vegetable garden things are burgeoning. I had a magnificent lunch of my first broccoli and spinach yesterday. They were so good. I have cultivated the garden. It looks great. The lettuces, all eaten by the rabbits in early May, came back and are ready to pick. Green blueberries are thick on the bushes. The asparagus is going to seed in a healthy manner, and so is the rhubarb. All around the vegetable garden area are tall, handsome, purple thistles and something that is almost Queen Anne's lace, but not quite. These days I eat breakfast and lunch out on the terrace while the sun streams down, the birds sing, and the scent of wild roses drifts up from my valley. It is lovely to go on a trip, but lovely to get home.

Joan came down for the weekend from Boston. She is feeling quite back to normal after her operation, and she was in excellent spirits, especially because of her marvelous new job in Los Gatos, California, with the Apple Computer Company. Through friends who work for this organization, Joan learned how it got its name. When the company was first started, the president was in a meeting with a group of his associates, thinking up a name for the firm. They were all having trouble. Finally, the president, who was peeling and eating an apple at the time, said, "If we haven't thought up a name in five minutes, we will call it the Apple Computer Company." And so it became.

I will, of course, miss Joan dreadfully when she moves in June, but we can change from our weekly phone calls to a lovely correspondence. I am so happy about the potential in her fine new job and her good feelings about everything. This compensates. We really have a lot to celebrate.

I will have to go to California again. After my last trip just a year ago to visit Bob and Tim and their families, I decided it was a long way and maybe that would be my last trip west. But now I wonder.

What is the message of June to me?
Maybe it is to loosen and let go and let summer take over.
W. H. Davies says, and again I turn to my quotes file from many years:

> What is this life if, full of care,
> We have no time to stop and stare?

These are the days to be lazy, to sit on the terrace with your favorite novel of the moment, if you like novels, and I do, or your favorite poetry book; to drowse, to read, to ruminate, to merely sit and be. Perhaps you will sip pineapple juice blended with a little mint and comfrey and eat homemade cookies and talk with your neighbor or friend who has dropped over. These are the days to shed all pressures, dispense with all rush. Don't crowd these summer weeks with musts. Instead, settle in the shade of a tree and write letters to your well-loved friends or family members. Being June, the weather is gentle. The days are soft, and one flows into another until you hardly remember what day of the week it is. Our bodies and spirits need a beautiful rest, and this is the month for it. Each week in June brings different flowers and shrubs into bloom; also different fragrances. June is the month of fragrances, I often think. After dinner I sit on the terrace and breathe in the various scents in my valley while I listen to Brahms's Fourth Symphony playing softly. The scent of Emily's and Frank's peonies comes my way. I am back from dinner now. It is quiet. I am alone and I am liking it. I am reminded of Cato, who wrote: "Never is one more active than when he does nothing, never is he less alone than when he is by himself."

Jane moves to Lancaster tomorrow to a retirement center called Lancashire Terrace. I drove over with her today to take a load of things and to see her apartment again, all papered and painted and with the pretty green carpet down. Its color matches the curtains we had chosen a couple of months ago. I will certainly miss her. It will be a new life for her and a good one, I am sure. She will come back frequently, she says. It is an hour away by car. She won't have a garden there until next year, and she plans to come back and work in mine this summer. Jane *has* to work in the soil. I will welcome her; so will my garden.

Last night it was clear and beautiful. I was walking alone along the rim of the valley outside my apartment. Overhead were myriad stars. Gradually, I began to feel at one with these stars that seemed so near, at one with the whole universe. It was a glorious feeling that quite transcended the moment. I was caught for a few minutes in a spell of enchantment and didn't want to come out of it.

But we always need to come back to earth. Earth is where we belong. It is nice, however, to have these moments of being lifted up out of our usual experiences. They present us with a small inner glow that is pleasant to live with.

When I came into the apartment I realized that, if I had been walking with someone, we probably would have been talking and would not have observed the stars in the same way. Probably we would have been commenting to each other on how beautiful they were, and we'd have been so busy talking *about* them we would not have received their messages. Our very comments would have kept us earthbound.

All this doesn't mean that I don't love to share perfect moments— a sunset, a moonrise, a beautiful flower, a vista—with a friend. I do, and any rich experience is doubled when you share it with someone you love. It is just that there are two separate ways of taking in— beauty observed alone and beauty observed with someone. We want some of each kind of experience in our lives—some aloneness and some appreciative moments with another or others.

There is a sunset viewing spot a few miles from here—an open area on a little rise. I often drive there with a friend to see the sun go down. We get there about a half hour ahead of time and watch all the preliminaries: the sky darkens, interesting colored clouds form, the line of trees in the foreground turns to dark silhouettes. The sky gradually comes to focus on the sun itself and its sinking out of sight. Sometimes it is so beautiful we are awed into silence and both of us merge with the beauty before us.

This morning I was kneeling on the hay in the sun in an enormous field where row after row of strawberries stretched. Beside me was a cardboard flat that I was enthusiastically filling with dark red, fully ripe, sun-warmed berries. Such a fragrance hovered over the field. Of course, now and then I must eat a berry. Every one tasted a little different and all were heavenly. What a morning!

Esther, Jane, and I had driven to Groff's Orchard near Oxford. We went through the Amish country where the clothes lines were hung with black garments and horses and buggies were tethered here and there. Occasionally we met a horse and buggy jogging along the road. Spreading over the banks of the highway grew solid masses of honeysuckle and wild lavender clover. Frequently, we passed a horse chestnut tree covered with lovely white flowers. We drove on Route 472 through beautiful farmland and rolling fields of corn a foot or so high. It was a sparkling day with brilliant sun and a cool breeze—a perfect June day.

At the orchard were a number of cars and people were already in the fields. Every few minutes a truck came by to take newcomers to the picking area. We all piled in one truck and off we went through vineyards, fields of ripe peas, cherry orchards. We decided we'd have to come back in September for grapes. But today was for strawberries. We were each assigned a row that stretched as far as we could see. We settled down on the hay between rows to pick. The berries were huge and glossy and well formed. Here we were with a long morning ahead of us in a beautiful spot where there was never a hurry. There were so many berries on each bush it was exciting to gather them.

After an hour or so we had enough berries. The flat was filled, our fingertips were pink, and our backs were ready to stop! We took the truck back to the big barn where they weighed the berries. I had ten and a half pounds. Jane and Esther had equally large amounts. We drove home in a glowing mood with the scent of strawberries filling the car. Jane stayed with me for lunch. She had come back from Lancaster for the picking.

I have already made a batch of individual shortcakes (using half whole wheat flour and half white flour), and they are in the freezer. Tomorrow I am having a dessert party and serving strawberry shortcake.

This afternoon I hulled the berries, washed them, put sugar on them, and set them in the refrigerator. Now I am all ready for tomorrow night. Of course I have many more berries than I can use, so I took some to neighbors in the building and to friends and to Edith in Firbank (the clinic section), where she is recovering from a fall. One of the real joys of summer is sharing garden produce with friends and neighbors.

Now I am on the terrace after supper, smelling the honeysuckle, listening to the music of the little song sparrow. We are better friends since he doesn't bang into my window anymore. The sun is setting, sending a rosy glow over the trees on the hillside across my valley. What peace descends!

How interesting and how much fun the last few days have been! Beginning with my dessert party. The fresh strawberry shortcake with lots of whipped cream was really delectable, and everyone seemed to like it. We met at the Center, all eight of us, four men and four women, and ate dinner together. Then everyone came over to my apartment. We began with a viewing of the garden. Some lilies of mysterious origins are all out, five of them, and so fragrant. These lilies dominate my little terrace garden, while the scent drifts in my bedroom window day and night. The purple clematis is sensational. The little annuals look perky and prim bordering the evergreens, and a slight breeze rustles the weeping birch.

Presently we all sat around the living room and ate shortcake and drank coffee and talked. Many interesting tales were told and ideas shared. It was a stimulating evening, leaving me much to think about when everyone went home and I was straightening things up.

Next morning Betty, a very good friend of mine from Tryon, North Carolina, arrived for a visit. Betty's husband died two weeks after Bob died. She and I grew to be close friends as we helped each other weather our difficult moments.

We had much news to catch up on. We talked and talked and then went for a swim. The oleanders at the pool are out, pink and yellow and red. It is truly beautiful there now, surrounded as it is by tropical plants, ferns, ivies, giant philodendrons, and other plants.

At the Quaker Birmingham Meeting House we sat out under the trees at long tables and had a delicious buffet supper, complete with homemade cookies. The weather made it a perfect day. Back at my apartment Betty and I settled on the terrace and conversed some more while the sun set and the scent of the lilies came our way. The fireflies made pricks of light against the cherry-tree foliage and through the air. I went to bed tonight not seeing stars tangled in the tree branches as I do in winter, but fireflies among the cherry-tree leaves.

We started the next day by hearing a fine sermon by Bob Young at the Westminster Presbyterian Church in West Chester.

This afternoon, after another good swim in our private tropic, we went over to Longwood Gardens. It was a time of roses there. Here was a circle made up of rose arbors all joined together and covered with American pillar roses in full flower. These are the deep pink, single ones shading to white at the centers. In the middle of the arbor circle stands a beautiful ornamental marble wellhead from Italy.

We sat on a bench to absorb the beauty of the roses for a while. Various other visitors strolled by. One attractive young couple walking hand in hand admired the roses for a few minutes, then came over and asked if we knew about cameras and if we would take a picture of them together in front of an arbor. I was delighted to do so.

In the rose garden proper were some very double garden party roses, cream touched with pink, that we fell in love with. And the peace roses were sensational. We walked about feeling, smelling, looking, and storing up memories to bring out and relive at auspicious moments.

Betty is especially interesting to go places with. She notices and appreciates everything. She called my attention to, among other things, the texture of the bark on a rare tree we passed and the intriguing nutlike seed pods on the paulownia trees above our heads. She doesn't miss a thing, and I love being with her.

Our last view of roses came as we were walking down a path bordered with large and ancient elms, at the end of which stood the circle of rose arbors with the American pillar roses; viewed from a distance, they were magnificent.

Our Spiritual Growth Group met today. Our subject was inner peace—its roots and fruits. Margaret led and did a fine job. We had a very thought-provoking discussion. I've been mulling it over ever since. What are the roots? What contributes to inner peace? Of course there are a number of factors, and if we each had a special list of what brings inner peace to us personally, all our lists might be different. Mine includes living my days free from rush and pressure, with intervals between events. Also, thinking positively. When your thoughts are constructive, how good you feel inside. Another contribution to inner peace for me is liking and accepting myself. If I am critical of myself and I don't like something I have done, I am not at peace within. Likewise, as you let go and let be, a great amount of serenity comes to you and stays. Equally so when you work in the garden.

If there is something we should do, but we keep putting it off, we don't feel at peace with ourselves. As soon as we force ourselves to do it, peace descends.

We talked about how desirable it is to have inner peace in the midst of confusion. This can be difficult, but worth struggling for. If you can create an island of peace within when you are surrounded by people who are upset, it can be a very growing experience. To realize that *we* don't have to be a part of the noise and confusion helps.

The fruits of inner peace, we agreed, are manifold. Something special emanates from you if you do have it, and people around you are aware of this and are drawn to you. Inner peace creates an atmosphere in a room or a house. Without knowing why, you like being there. Inner peace is a quality we have intermittently. I guess no one of us has it constantly.

At the end of the discussion, we all felt inner peace was something worth thinking about and working toward.

I've been thinking about Joan off and on all day and can't get her off my mind. This is the day she flies to California. I talked to her on the phone last night, and she was tremendously excited. She said she had a sense of unreality about it all. It seemed as if it was happening to someone else—all the packing, shipping the car, sending the furniture by van, farewell parties by all her special friends, a final canoe trip on the Charles River with a particular friend. And now she is off. She must be over Kansas by now. It is a beautiful day for flying.

Joan starts her job next Monday. She said it was going to be so interesting she could hardly wait to begin. She will be in a motel for a week or so until she finds a place to live. I am wishing her happiness in her new venture. I have been sending her special good wishes all day long.

I've been poring through Wayside Garden's last fall catalog, looking at pictures of lilies to see if I could find my fabulous lily. I believe I have solved the mystery; not of where it came from—that mystery remains—but of what it is. I'm just about sure it is a regal lily. It exactly resembles the picture. I feel better to be able to give it a name. It has been beautiful all month, filling my outdoors with a very sweet fragrance, and my bedroom, too. I am going to order a few more this fall and plant them in the terrace garden between the chrysanthemums. They will be dramatic and lovely there.

Some of the day lilies Jane and Helen planted on the bank last fall for my birthday are budding and blooming, and all flourish. The wild, orange day lilies along the roadsides in the area are flowering in profusion and are lovely. The blue chickory also borders the road to town. Around the edges of Crosslands the lavender vetch originally planted here is full out and truly spectacular as it grows in tumbling masses. Here and there as you drive about you discover banks of pink roses, probably escaped. This is a garden month for sure. We have had several good showers, so things are very green and growing madly. My lettuces and spinach have been and are superb. String beans are thriving, but not ready to eat yet. The garden peas ripen more every day, and I pick them by the basketful, share some with neighbors, eat them for lunch, and freeze some. They are delectable. I had cooked some of my fresh gathered peas and wrapped them in two aluminum foil packages and last night when I had dinner with Esther at the Center we each had a serving with our dinner. They were still hot and heavenly! Not the conventional thing to do perhaps, but very satisfying.

Today I baked a chocolate angel cake for another dessert party tomorrow night. I was in the middle of stirring everything when I discovered I had none of the cocoa the recipe calls for. I had to stop and go to the Acme and get some. The cake rose up gloriously and is cooling upside down now on a ginger-ale bottle.

Alas, dresses are getting shorter and I have to shorten all of mine. What a project! And I like them longer too. Oh hum! I think I will start and do one this afternoon sitting on the terrace. Will the mockingbird be singing in the wild cherry tree while I sew?

This is one of those days when I do many practical, useful things: washing, baking, watering and weeding the garden (which doesn't take long since it is so small), and picking peas. I like a day of this sort now and then. I feel so good at the end of it when I realize how many different jobs I've accomplished. Maybe I'll go for a swim now before I do my first hem.

These days, every individual is pulled in many directions. This is not good, but neither do we want to close ourselves off. We must be open to family, friends, home, community, and national interests. We all have our special personal concerns that involve us, stimulate us, and enrich our lives. While being responsive, we cannot go in every direction that draws us. We must discriminate, for we want to remain whole and balanced in the midst of the many ways we are drawn. We need to have an inner core of quiet and steadiness. We read of distant suffering in crowded cities, wars in far places. Always there are world troubles and needs that draw us; and nearer home there are intimate friends in trouble, family complications. We must not diffuse ourselves, fragment our lives. If we do, we are useless to ourselves and others. How do we avoid it?

We all have our special ways of remaining in balance and whole and keeping our serenity. For me one way is working in the garden, keeping close to the soil indoors and out.

Plants grow at their own pace, mature at the right season. There is a steadiness that comes to you when you work in the soil. Everything in nature happens at its right moment. This you learn, along with many other things, as you grow a garden. With your hands in the earth a great peace comes to you.

Gardening is participation in nature's beauty. Often there is a kind of awe that you feel in the garden. A kind of reverence comes over you sometimes when you have your hands in the soil, as you dig and plant and cultivate and water, and as you watch things grow from day to day.

I have always felt that, if you keep your feet on the ground, your hands in the earth, and your head among the stars, you'd be all right no matter what.

10❀

July Is Accepting

July comes in on a note of violence. In the late afternoon of the first day of the month the sky clouded over, growing darker and darker. After supper a great wind arose and blew the tree branches every which way. All through my valley the trees tossed madly in the gale. Great black clouds swept across a turbulent sky. Now and then a clap of thunder sounded, growing nearer and louder as the storm approached. A terrace chair blew over, and small branches ripped out of the cherry tree down onto the lawn. I stood outside the living room glass doors watching the storm. I was hypnotized by it.

There is something thrilling about observing the wild forces of nature loose themselves over the landscape. The storm gathered strength, and every few moments I noticed a difference. All at once I felt within me a kind of tingling, as if a responding force were gathering, stirred by the violence without, something that echoed the forces already raging. There was for a few instants the sense that a part of me was related in some way to the heart of the storm.

Then the rain descended and I came indoors. It lashed hard against the closed windows and poured down the flagstone terrace. Through the darkening valley, sweeps of rain blew in great drifts. This went on, wind and rain, thunder and lightning, for a while. Glued to the living room glass doors, I lost all sense of time. I was stirred to my depths by all these elements loosed without and felt a close part of it all.

As quickly as it had come, the rain subsided, the thunder moved off, the wind slowed, and the sky over the valley developed a reddish hue. Then as I stepped out onto the terrace I saw it, a great arching rainbow right over Crosslands, one end anchored in the buildings and the other lost in the treetops of my valley.

And so July is here, ushered in with a storm and a promise.

My fingers smell wonderful. I have just finished trimming the chrysanthemums back to five inches, and the leaves are so fragrant. This is the third and last cutting for them. I began this spring when they had reached six inches and I cut them to four inches. Then a second time, when they were about eight inches tall, I cut them to five inches. And now the last time. My goal is to have them bloom when the plants are low and don't need staking. My system of three trimmings is supposed to attain this end. Will it?

It is lovely out tonight, a cool breeze rustling the leaves on the trees. The last birds—a wren, a song sparrow, and a thrush—are singing, each his own song. I will sit out on my terrace and watch dusk fall. The grass was cut yesterday, and it looks neat and trim. I clipped around the edges tonight, and that adds the finishing touch. As dusk falls the last beams of a setting sun streak across the trees on the far side of the valley, tinting them a warm rose hue. Soon this fades. The day is over and my fingers still smell of chrysanthemums.

I love it when the rain bounces on my terrace flagstones, creating little interlacing circles of water, and on the pavement when I am driving. This is how it is today. A real good old rainy day. Ever since our drought last year, rain makes me very happy. We have had a lot of it in the last weeks, and the drought problems are just about over. The grass everywhere is very green. The corn fields in the farm area around us are growing furiously and are a very rich deep green, too. The fields of wheat are ripe and gold in the sun. The leaves on the trees are lush and thick. All gardens everywhere are flourishing.

Last night, after I got in bed, I heard for the first time the lovely music of the cicadas and other summer insects. The night before last all was quiet. Then last night they began. I wonder what makes them come so suddenly. How do they know that July third is the night to begin? And do they always begin on July third? I'll have to remember to check next year. It is a comfortable summer sound regardless of dates and the ways of insects, and I like it.

The seed pods of the clematis are pure enchantment. The vine climbs the brick wall of my building on both sides of the bedroom windows. The tangled green pods hang in clusters, and I see them whenever I look out the windows. They are round and symmetrical and feel a little springy when I cup one in my hand. They are about two and a half inches in diameter and are put together in spirals.

One year when the pods turned brown and were thoroughly dry in the fall I planted some seeds in a pot in my window. It took several sowings before they sprouted and grew, but they finally did, and I gave the plants to Esther and Bob. The whole side wall of their terrace is now covered with clematis vines and deep blue blooms every May.

Last night Jane came over from Lancaster for the night. We sat on the terrace and watched fireflies until bedtime. She sleeps on my sofa bed when she comes. We took a walk in the rain this morning with raincoats, hats, and umbrellas. The sound of the rain on the umbrellas was a delight. We were the only people out. It was lovely.

We had a very festive Fourth of July dinner—a choice between filet mignon and fresh salmon at the Center. It was fun to see Jane, and we had a lot to catch up on. She is really very happy in Lancaster, and I am so pleased.

This day of solid rain reminds me of a delightful poem by Frances Shaw in *The Quiet Eye*:

> Who loves the rain,
> And loves his home,
> And looks on life with quiet eyes,
> Him will I follow through the storm:
> And at his hearth fire keep me warm;
> Nor hell nor heaven shall that soul surprise
> Who loves the rain,

And loves his home,
And looks on life with quiet eyes.
—Untitled

My new African violet plants are on the living room floor by the windows. They are flourishing. It is supposed to take the plants a year to bloom after they have been put in water. Will they meet their schedule and flower in August? I wonder.

What is the message of July? To me it is the need for acceptance. We need to accept the heat as it streams over the land. We need to accept the creatures ever busy eating our lettuces and broccoli; the Japanese beetles that fly up from the grass onto our legs when we walk to the Center. We need to take action first—sprays, etc.—then accept. The things we cannot take action on or solve we need to accept from the start. There are always plenty of these.

Today's meeting of our Spiritual Growth Group was on the subject of acceptance. What a vast and fascinating subject it turned out to be.

We discussed the three kinds of acceptance: of yourself, of others, of situations.

Most everyone in the group agreed that it was difficult to accept yourself, that we all tended to downgrade ourselves. Why?

One way of helping to accept yourself, we agreed, was to think of specific things you like about yourself, successful moments you have had. Instead of dwelling on errors, dwell more on the times things have worked out well for you. We can't love ourselves if we don't accept ourselves. We have to accept our shadow selves as well. If we don't love ourselves, it is difficult to love another.

What do you do when a close friend or family member decides to do something that you see as a big mistake? Do you quietly accept or do you protest? How much responsibility do we have to our own integrity? Should we be honest and speak up to our friend or relative, or should we let him go his own way? I don't believe there is any answer to this. All such situations are difficult. The only thing we can do is follow our own inner guidance with each such situation. If the person making a mistake is an adult, then we have to question seriously if we can have any effect. Besides, we could be wrong. How can we be sure we are right in our judgment?

Acceptance is a spiritual, emotional, and mental experience.

Acceptance is the way to wholeness. It is necessary at every separate step on the way and in every relationship in our world.

If there is something we cannot accept, then we need to accept our nonacceptance.

Maybe we can't change events, but we can change our attitudes toward them and our responses. Thus, for us, they change from difficult experiences to ones we can accept.

In our relationships and friendships acceptance is basic and vital. My friend and I touch each other with a part of each of our minds. Then there are other areas where we see things very differently, where we don't touch at all. To build a successful relationship, we have to accept these differences and relate in the areas where we do touch.

In world situations where there is not one positive action we can take, we will sleep better at night and be more serene and balanced if we accept things as they are. When there is nothing we can do to change the course of events, acceptance is the most positive action we can take.

Acceptance is bad when we sit in a heap in the midst of a bad situation that could be improved, and we take no steps to improve it, no steps to get ourselves out of some muddle we have gotten into. This is acceptance at its worst. There is a time to walk on and a time to take action. Sometimes only our inner guidance will help us differentiate.

I woke to the businesslike sound of the lawn mower and that delicious summer scent of fresh-cut grass. How heavy the air was, heavy with humidity, and the temperature on my terrace was in the mid-eighties. The sun beat down relentlessly. This is the day not to move fast or hurry.

I drove to town, and all along the roadside were countless wild-flowers. Snowy white Queen Anne's lace stood tall and dignified. Next to its feathery foliage were groups of dainty, low-growing but-ter-and-eggs. And just beyond was a great sweep of black-eyed Susans gilding a meadow. Nearby was a bank of lavender vetch. In town along the highway, clusters of deep sky-blue chickory enhanced the scene. And some escaped hollyhocks reached up next to the furry seed pods of the purple thistles, so lovely last month.

I returned books to the library, mailed packages, and stopped at Heritage Gardens to get a spray for leaf minor, which is what my weeping birch is suffering from. Then back home to my blessed air-conditioned apartment. I could feel my rapidly evaporating energy re-turn after a few minutes indoors, while outside the window the tem-perature had risen to ninety-five in the shade.

We're in a heat wave.

The heat rises up from the ground when you walk over to the Center and feels hot on your legs. The heat shimmers through the air; it bounces off the buildings and wraps around you. It presses down on you all over as soon as you step outside the door. There is a blue heat haze over the valley. It is midsummer, and this is how it is. Getting along with and making your peace with rising temperatures and humidity is a part of summer, a part of accepting, a part of the message of July.

Actually, we are very comfortable here with our air-conditioning in our apartments and in the Center. It is a time to hole in, write let-ters, read, and relax. I decided to clear out all my kitchen cupboards this month, just one or two each day, and dust all the books in my book cases, and go over the closets gradually.

This is not the time to go outdoors except to go quickly from here to there. It is not the time to sit and eat lunch on the terrace, pull a weed, or even go near the vegetable garden in the hollow. I have zinnias to pick there, beans, peas, and lettuces to harvest, but they will have to wait. I will groom my indoors and brave the out-doors to have a daily swim; but no mile walk in this weather. I'll catch up on my letters, read my library books. Then I had the happy thought of inviting people over for fruit juice, ginger preserves, cream cheese sandwiches, and cake. I've a sponge cake I made in the freezer. I asked a different person each afternoon all week, someone I had not asked to my apartment before and had never really talked to. This was so interesting and stimulating. I got to know better some very special people I had not known before. It turned out to be particularly enjoyable.

Last night I went over to Kendal to eat dinner with Elizabeth and Helen. We had such a good time talking and dining together. We hatched up a beautiful plan. Elizabeth doesn't mind driving long distances, and she said she'd love to drive the two of us to the shore, to Stone Harbor, and we'd have a day at the beach being cooled by ocean breezes, breathing in salt air and taking a picnic lunch. We all got carried away with the idea and could think of nothing else. We picked a day a week off.

Today, in the practical light of early morning and the heat of a new day, we began to realize that it might be a lot better to go in the fall when it was cooler. We all communed by phone and agreed, so this is something nice to look forward to for the three of us.

Cheers! Our heat wave is over. It is cool enough so that the sun is welcome, and there is a lovely breeze. I went down to the vegetable area this morning with a large basket and scissors and picked dozens of zinnias in all colors. I filled the apartment with them— a bouquet in every room. They are bright and gay and dazzling in the places where they stand. I also harvested the last peas, the first string beans, and some broccoli. My lunch was dreamy, a heaping plate of three vegetables. They were delectable.

I took a bouquet of zinnias over to Edith in Firbank, the clinic section of the medical wing. I carried a large armful to Sally and left them in water outside her apartment door, as she was out. How pleasant it always is to share garden produce with friends. My little vegetable garden needs some loving care. The peas need pulling up, and there are a number of weeds all through it. The tomatoes are burgeoning and covered with ripening green fruit. I was glad to see my garden again. I have missed it during the heat wave. But the gardens are in a low spot where there is seldom a breeze. It is a good growing place, but far from cool these days.

I particularly like to shop in the months of July and August. There are so many wonderful fruits to choose from. Today, among the usuals, there were peaches, bing cherries, canteloupes, honeydews, and blueberries. They smell so good that I can never resist. I have a favorite summertime luncheon and Sunday-supper dish. You take a bowl of cottage cheese, cover it with fresh blueberries, pour milk on top, and sprinkle with brown sugar. This is a most filling and thinning meal, and I love it.

Summer is a lovely time of year, barring the occasional heat waves. I am outdoors so much. In the morning, first thing before I do anything, I like to step out on the terrace and see what has grown overnight. I like to move out onto the ground and feel the earth through my slippers. The early-morning air is so fresh. Birds are singing. A little dew lingers in the grass. Some new platycodon flowers are out. I pick off the dead heads of yesterday's blooms. My chrysanthemums have grown a little. They are flourishing since my last trim back. There is something rather wonderful about the beginning of a new day. What will I do with this precious gift of today? What will it do with me?

The last thing before I go to bed I like to step out again. Evenings are as cool and fresh as mornings, and the earth feels good to stand upon. I once heard about a man living in New York City in an apartment house on the tenth floor. He had a box of earth in which he used to stand barefoot for minutes morning and night. He believed that this contact with the earth kept him balanced and healthy. I often wonder. I don't know about the health angle, but I enjoy my last contact with the earth at the end of the day as well as at the beginning. Evening in the garden is a very special time. As dusk descends the white flowers stand out, while the brightly colored ones fade into the evening. And then the moon rises. The fireflies prick their way through the gloaming. The evening insects begin their intermittent music. The garden shapes, bushes and such, stand out in interesting patterns in the moonlight. Maybe it is a starlit night. There is so much sky here at Crosslands. Any kind of night is rather lovely. We see so many stars—all my favorite constellations. I enjoy picking them out. After a warm day there is a particular summer-evening scent that drifts through the garden. If you have just watered, the summer-evening scent is stronger. I do enjoy the refreshment of a few minutes in the garden walking on the earth and looking up at the stars before I go to bed.

Summer days slide slowly by—long, lazy days of picking beans in the garden and armsful of zinnias, broccoli, and lettuces. I harvest for my friends as well as myself. My lunches are mostly from the garden these days. Picking beans, crisp and green, down on my knees while the wild geese fly over and the insects sing in the grass is a pleasant pastime. I drove down to Woodward's farm this morning to buy my first just-picked sweet corn.

These are the days for swimming in a leisurely way up and down the pool. Each day I do my eighth of a mile. Recently we had a moonlight swim party. The lights glimmered on the water, creating a romantic effect as we swam about. All my swim friends were there. Standing on the brink of the pool, we drank lemonade and ate delectable cookies. The only thing lacking was the full moon! It was a cloudy evening with no moon at all. But it was warm, and the swim cooled us all off.

It is hot and humid. Reading, writing letters, and relaxing are the best pastimes. I don't much like the heat, but this we have to accept. It is the season for it. We need to accept the dryness too. Every day lately is sunny and clear. I water my garden frequently after dinner before dark.

Yesterday Sally and I drove over to Lancaster to see Jane and spend the day with her. Coming back, we stopped at a roadside stand

and each bought a fabulous large melon. It smelled heavenly and was simply delicious when I ate some of it this morning.

How we all avoid the word *death*, and anything about it, in early and mid-life. Then, as we grow older, we cease to have such an aversion to the mention of the word. When someone you love dies, you feel still different. You begin to make your peace with death.

Perhaps it may seem odd to some people to think about death in July when all the earth is burgeoning with life. But here in Crosslands the point of view on the subject, gathered from the few I have discussed it with, is very different and very healthy. Most people here believe as I do, that death is not an end at all but a change and the beginning of a new life, the entrance to a continued existence. Since I know I will meet those I love again when I die, there is no dread attached to the whole idea, but a pleasant acceptance. Not that I sit around thinking about death. But when a thought of it crosses my mind, I envision it as a great moment and a new adventure. I have enjoyed all the great moments of my life: falling in love, my wedding day, the birth of each of my children, the new era when they all left home and my husband and I were alone again, retirement. And now I fully expect to enjoy death.

I think what we all fear and dread is a long and painful illness leading to death; but actually dying, passing from one state of being to another, will be an extremely momentous occasion. I'd rather it didn't come this year; I have things I want to do. You see, I am very fond of living and find life as I get older becoming richer each year as I learn a little more and grow a little more. But when death does come I shall be ready for it. You can never know ahead of time your reactions to any occurrences, so I can't guarantee my response; but this is how it seems to me I will feel in the light of my present point of view. I don't dwell on this subject or think very much about it, but when it happens I think I shall be ready. I wonder.

There have been serious studies on parapsychology in a number of countries, with remarkable results. These studies seem to indicate that there is life after death; but as yet we have no definite proof. Can we

ever have real proof? Do we need it? I believe what I believe and feel
no need of further confirmation or proof. Before she died, Pearl
Buck, that wise elderly woman, wrote about the dragonfly, which
seems to me to relate in a rather wonderful way.

> When my small children could not understand the silence
> between their recently dead father and us who loved him so
> dearly, I explained by describing to them the life cycle of the
> dragonfly. It begins as a grub in water. Then at the proper mo-
> ment, it surfaces and finds it has wings and flies away.
> "I suppose," I told them, "that the ones left in the water
> wonder where he went and why he doesn't come back. But he
> can't because he has wings. Nor can they go to him because
> they don't have wings yet."

Pearl Buck went on to say, "Something like that is true, I believe.
We haven't our wings yet either. But some day?"

Meanwhile, I do believe this life here and now is beautiful enough
to need no distant heaven for its justification. Heaven in all its summertime of beauty is with us right now, surging up to our very feet,
reaching out to touch our hearts. But do we always know how to al-
low it to enter?

11❄

August Is Blessings

August is the month of harvest and of plenty. All along the roadsides are fruit stands piled high with sweet corn, peaches, blueberries, melons, squashes, and countless other fruits and vegetables. In the fields of our area the corn is high and lush, with green waving tassels at the top. Along the roadsides the butterfly weed unfolds its orange blooms. There are sweeps of wild, pink sweet peas everywhere. The goldenrod stalks are beginning to show color. Masses of purple spires rise up out of the roadside grasses. I couldn't find the names of these in my wildflower book. No matter, they are lovely, and I stopped by the edge of the pavement and picked a large armful.

Everywhere gardens are fulfilling themselves. Last month we battled the wild creatures, blights, and insects; this month it is too late. What is done is done. We don't worry, but enjoy what is left, and that is plenty. The vegetable gardens in Crosslands are lush with all kinds of produce. People come down every day with baskets to reap their harvest and share their surplus. In the various buildings are baskets of ripe tomatoes, zucchini, squash, and cucumbers, each with a sign that reads "Help Yourself."

Days are a bit shorter, and nights a little cooler. Stars are numerous and bright. Often, evenings are spent on the terrace enjoying a cooling breeze. It is midsummer, a time of freedom and relaxation, and a holiday feeling abounds.

In my garden tomatoes are ripening—reds and yellows, since I have both kinds. When they are picked warm with the sun on them and eaten on the spot, they are delectable. And the scent of the foliage is everywhere. It is one of my favorite summer fragrances. Salad lunches are in order these days, lunches on the terrace when it is cool enough.

I live with zinnias in the apartment—all over it. Sometimes the flower committee takes some to decorate the Center. A favorite bouquet of mine is zinnias with Queen Anne's lace. The latter is abundant in our fields now.

The terrace gardens of Crosslands residents are flourishing, too. In the evenings people take walks to see them, passing along the grass beyond our terraces. If I am sitting out I have the fun of talking with those who come. It becomes a pleasant, sociable time, a time of compliments and good feelings all around.

What an exciting moment! I went to water my African violet seedlings this morning after breakfast, and there, nestled down among the leaves at the center of one plant, were three uncurling stems with pink flower buds on them. So it is true, then, what I had been told, that it takes a year from the time you put a leaf stem in water to the first bloom.

I have a total of six young plants now. I started out with ten leaves. All rooted, but after planting them and having them grow several months, I kept only the six strongest. I wonder if they will all bloom this month. The five parent plants they are replacing look even more decrepit than last fall. It will be good to have the strong young ones in their stead. Several of the new ones have more than one plant in a pot. I will divide them when I repot them this fall.

This is the first time I have tried propagating African violets from a leaf, and I am terribly proud of my results. I have quite a maternal feeling about these young plants. It is a very good sensation when you have cooperated with Nature to create a few altogether new plants. It is on a par with how you feel when you plant a seed and it comes up—a simple enough experience, but thrilling each time you do it.

All gardening is really cooperating with Nature, and I can't think of a more worthwhile occupation, or one that is more just plain fun and stimulating.

Sometimes ancient sayings have just as much meaning now as they did when first used. "Count your blessings" is one such example. It is a particularly good thing to do when you get a little low-spirited. Most of us do have down moments from time to time. Count your blessings is the message coming to us from August. Being the harvest season, many good things come our way from the earth—and also from life, if we stop to think about it. How rewarding it is to think about our many blessings. Whoever we are and however many things in our lives give us troubles, it could always be worse. And if we sit and think a while we can find many blessings in our lives. When we review these, we do ourselves a favor, a large favor. We bring positive forces to bear in our lives. A great deal of power comes from inviting positive thoughts into the mind.

So while we recognize counting our blessings as an ancient and old-fashioned custom, it is one that is just as valuable and constructive today. Although any month is a good time to do this, August seems especially appropriate, with our blessings from the gardens so numerous, with the gardens completing themselves and filled to overflowing with abundance. It seems natural to be counting our blessings in other areas at the same time.

I believe that the older we grow the more meaningful family relationships become to us, the more we enjoy being with family, getting letters from them and phone calls. Not that we don't enjoy all these contacts when we and they are younger; but we find them particularly heartwarming during our later years. Kay and I telephone each other every couple of weeks or so. We are the two oldest members of our family. There is something especially compatible about close relatives our own age.

Then, of course, children are so wonderful to hear from. Their letters mean so much. I look forward all day and have a good feeling inside when I know Joan is going to phone me in the evening. I enjoy every moment of her call when it comes, and afterward I coast off to sleep ruminating on all we have discussed. Children, when they become middle-aged, are so interesting with their added depth, their deeper understanding, and their mature wisdom.

All my three children are in California now, very far away. I don't get out there too often, and they seldom come east. So letters and phone calls are our means of communicating.

I have a lovely time corresponding with some of my grandchildren. I have six, four in California and two in New England. Would I could see more of them. But this is how life is for some of us. Miles separate us. And there is nothing to be done about it. Here is where acceptance comes into the picture again. We need to learn to accept this distance and get along with the reality of the situation, just as we need to learn to enjoy our occasional phone calls and letters.

I get lonesome for my family sometimes and really long to see and be with them. That is how it was this afternoon. Now, after supper tonight, I feel a kind of ache and a heaviness all over. I am used to this feeling. It is just my "missing family" feeling. It comes once in a while.

I sat down to cope and began by writing letters. Not to my family. They owe me letters, and I always wait to hear from them before answering. I don't want to shower them with several letters at once that they must answer, so I respond to them, then wait until I hear before writing again. Instead, I caught up on other mail, and wrote to friends in faraway places. This was a help for a while. I went for a walk to the Center to mail my letters. When I returned I pulled weeds in the terrace garden. Then I went in and called Kay. We talked for several minutes. I could sense the phone bill rising, and I couldn't care less. We just went on talking.

Now dusk is descending, the fireflies appearing. I will bathe and get in bed with my book and read until it is time to go to sleep. I love reading in bed. It is so comfortable with pillows and all.

I was reading happily when the phone rang; the call was from

Joan. She is settled in her new house and loves it. She is part way up a mountain with views in all directions. She finds her job most interesting, had friends for dinner tonight, and is very happy. Her call dispersed the last of my low-moment ache, and I drifted off to sleep contented. Isn't it amazing how our moods change and what incidents change them? Different incidents with each of us, I'm sure.

Last night I woke up in the middle of the night with a dreadful pain on the left side of my forehead and the left side of the back of my head. It was so bad I couldn't think straight. I got up and heated a cup of milk and a couple of teaspoons of molasses, my usual sleep-inducing drink, and sipped this. After sitting up a while my headache lessened. I went back to bed and promptly to sleep. I concluded it was just one of those mysterious things that happen to us for no good reason. All is well today, so I guess it is nothing to worry about. I won't think about it anymore.

When I first came to Crosslands it used to bother me to see people in wheelchairs or with canes or crutches. I would wonder if someday I might have their problems. One day I went to see Lloyd Lewis about it. He is the director of Kendal-Crosslands (the two are sister communities that adjoin each other). Lloyd, I assumed, would have developed some philosophy about this situation because dealing with the physically handicapped was part of his job.

He was very understanding about my attitude and explained that, as he got to know a person, the obvious physical problems no longer disturbed him at all. In fact, he became unaware of them. This bit of wisdom certainly helped me a great deal. Then, over the months, something else occurred. I began to see, not the difficulties, but the courage of these people. Of course I never got to know all those who have physical problems, only a few. But whether or not I know them, it no longer disturbs me to see them about. I am so impressed by their stamina and strength of character and courage and just plain guts.

For example, Edith, since her fall, is confined to a wheelchair and will be for some time. Sally and I went to see her yesterday afternoon. Sally began asking her about some of her physical problems. Edith said, a little impatiently, "I don't want to talk about them. What is just is, and that is all there is to it."

So we spoke of other things. Edith is so brave and has such courage to face what she does every day of her life and to do it with a smile, all the while joking with and reassuring those who come to take care of her.

This harvest month is a good time to look back at the garden since it started growing in the spring and evaluate. My vegetable garden has been productive; there are huge quantities of peas (some in the freezer) and lettuces, in spite of predators, broccoli, beans, and parsley. I have all the tomatoes my friends and neighbors and I can eat. And there are so many zinnias.

Indoors is the excitement of the African violets. Three more plants have buds on them. I can't tell their colors yet, but they are there!

The asparagus was the one crop failure. There was only a handful of edible stalks. But the greenery now is lush and abundant due to plenty of plant food, so surely by next year there will be a good crop. There I go being a typical gardener, living in the future as well as the present and past!

The crop that promises to be sensational and is yet to come is fall raspberries. The plants are green and healthy and tall and are spreading all over the place. I pruned them too heavily in the late winter and so no spring berries; but as if to make up for this, they are preparing a bumper crop for this fall.

This morning I was out in the garden picking dead heads off my large and beautiful platycodon plant. It has been blooming about six weeks now. These are almost the last of the blossoms for this year. This plant will then rest quietly in the garden until next summer. Meanwhile, on both sides of it are chrysanthemums. Looking carefully at the many leaved stalks on these, I noticed deep down in the heart of all the top leaves the very beginning of flower buds—the first I have seen.

As one plant passes its blooming period it ushers in another getting ready to start flowering. And so it goes. It is like this in our lives, too. As one period of living ends, another commences. Can we always be ready to recognize the new period and welcome it and, at the same time, loose and let go of the one that is passing?

Jane and I set forth in the car at nine o'clock in the morning yesterday. We were in a carefree mood and had planned to drive to Ocean City on the New Jersey shore for the day. We had our lunch and a jug of water and bathing suits. It was *the* day of the summer to go because it was cool and clear and sunny. We drove along past miles of New Jersey pine trees and then came into a peach-orchard section. On both sides of the road were rows and rows of peach trees, from very young ones to completely mature ones. The peaches had been harvested. How lovely that road would be in the spring when they were all flowering. We drove on for a couple of hours, and when we were almost there, we crossed a causeway and got our first wonderful whiff of salt air. Salt marshes surrounded us. Finally we arrived at the beach. It was a beautiful stretch of sand, gay with many colored umbrellas, people by the dozens, and sand castles that were marvelous constructions. Children with small pails of water wandered about.

We settled at one end of the beach and watched the breakers a while. They were very gentle and the water very blue. The lovely smell of salt air surrounded us. How content you can be just sitting watching and listening to waves. And then there were gulls swooping about so gracefully. Everything at the beach seemed serene and filled with the joyous feeling of a holiday. There were parents of young children, groups of women, and many devoted young couples. We were a little apart from the crowd, which appeared as a foreground for the view of the ocean, gulls, cloudless sky, and white, white sand. Wading out to swim, we saw a friendly crab or two and bits of green seaweed. The water was clear and clean and cold! After the Crosslands pool, kept at about eighty-five degrees, it seemed like ice; but we braved it and ducked under. How delightful saltwater feels on the skin! I tingle all over after I have been in it. I never want to wash it off.

We sat in the shade of the boardwalk on the hard, white sand and ate our sandwiches, watching waves, other swimmers, small children running in the shallows, and still other children building those fabulous sand castles. It all seemed like a painting by a French impressionist, maybe Seurat. We, as part of the painting, seemed in a delicious dream world. And we loved it. I don't know how long we sat there. Time ceased to exist. But finally the moment came to leave and drive back. We made the long drive through New Jersey again, with its peach orchards and pines and arrived at Crosslands thoroughly relaxed and filled with salt air and the spirit of a holiday. It is so refreshing to take off for somewhere else for a while. I felt as if I had been away for days! I was a little hazy through dinner and went to bed early.

I picked the last of my beans this morning before it got too hot. This was the day of a great feast. Bea came for dinner, and we were having fresh lobster. The White Barn has lobsters, and they cooked them and cracked them for us. I picked them up just before dinner. Bea had made heavenly zucchini soup to serve cold first. We ate by candlelight, which is always glamorous. We dunked the lobster in hot melted butter, and it was pure ambrosia! Such a pleasant occasion, and afterward we sat on the terrace and watched dusk descend. Then Bea, bless her heart, helped me do the dishes. I like eating at home occasionally where it is quiet and where I can have something really special. I also love to cook and like to keep my hand in.

Today is the day of the Harvest Festival here at Crosslands, a festival for the display of anything grown in the gardens, anything in the line of vegetables, that is. About noon, people began bringing in their entries. There were three long tables on three sides of the auditorium. All were covered with attractive green cloths. There were a variety of classes, seventeen in all, that included many different kinds of vegetables, herbs, harvest arrangements, and gourds.

What beautiful produce people came up with! There were luscious, large tomatoes, raspberries, beautiful eggplants, enormous zucchini squash. One weighing ten pounds won the prize for the largest. I never saw such handsome potatoes. Mushrooms were in evidence, too, large, snowy white puff balls, and cucumbers, and yellow squash, green peppers with their shiny skins, and delectable, red rhubarb stalks. Of course we all oohed and ahed over each other's produce. We also looked and felt. Eggplants are so nice to touch. So are many of the other vegetables exhibited. Several people had entered braids of onions. Fresh, healthy vegetables have such a live, firm feeling and such a look of vitality about them.

Everyone was in a good mood. There were many prizes. Practically everyone won something, which made all the entrants happy. A little healthy competition is stimulating, and all those who grow vegetables participated. All who came to the festival had a good time.

Our Harvest Festival represents the climax of this productive garden year. Of course we will continue to have garden vegetables, continue to share our tomatoes and zucchini squash and other surplus. We will go on enjoying our own home-grown food for several weeks to come. But all the same, the season is drawing to a close.

After I got home from the festival I watched a large, orange full moon rise up over my valley. I sat on the terrace a while listening to a few late birds sing. Soon the evening insects began their nightly serenade, while the subtle scent of white petunias drifted my way and mingled with the fragrance of the white nicotiana next door.

August nights are lovely. They are often cool and fresh, and the grass, damp with dew, has a special midsummer smell.

For five nights in a row now I have wakened at about two A.M. with that dreadful headache. It is better by day, but never gone, and terrible in the night. The doctor, after doing a thorough examination and giving me a number of pills, ordered sinus X-rays, and all was normal there. Now the plan is to go next week and have a brain scan to be sure there is no tumor. When I considered this possibility I became quite panicky, especially in the middle of the night when I had such pain. I don't believe you think very clearly at two A.M., especially when you are in pain. All coherent thought leaves you. You feel shaky inside, very much alone, and faith is hard to come by. Mostly you are enveloped in panic and fear. At least I was.

Jane has been sleeping here on my sofa bed the last few nights. It was certainly a lifesaver having her. When you have a bad pain you simply can't get away from it. There it is, and there you are, and it seems as if never the twain will part. It is good to have company. In the cold light of this morning, when I heard that the sinus X-rays were normal and that I was to have a brain scan on Monday, I began to think more clearly.

I believe that, in a difficult situation, you have to consider the worst possibility, live with it for a while, view it from all angles, and then see how you can improve it. Then you have to do the best you can with it.

So, I thought, suppose I do have a tumor on the brain and have it operated on and die. Well, it is over quickly and this is what I pray for when my time comes—that I do not linger with a terrible ailment. Also, if I die, I will be with Bob. Merely thinking about this gives me great comfort. Whenever death is a possibility I believe you have to face it and make your peace with it. I can make my peace with death now if I have to, but it isn't quite as easy as I thought. However, I have lived a long and full life, a wonderful life, in fact. How much better it is to go now, if I must, when I have had a fine last year and last months, and when I am at peace with all living things, all people, and am thoroughly content. I have things I wanted to do this next year, but I suppose this is how it will always be. There will never be a perfect time to leave this life.

Now, what is the good side of the picture? What are the blessings attached to the situation, if any? I have a doctor I like and trust, and I am sure I am in good hands. The hospitals here are good. And, best of all, suppose I turn out not to have any tumor at all? Suppose the cause of the problem is something quite different? It has felt better today than any day since the problem arose. Suppose it clears up by itself with the help of the pills I am taking? This could happen. And in a month I will be going my merry way, having forgotten completely my near brush with death–at least with the idea of death.

So at this point I have put myself in God's hands. If I have to go I'll try to go gracefully. If I don't have to, so much the better. The hope I am dwelling with through this day without pain and will continue to live with is the hope that I do not have a tumor, do not need an operation. Either way, I can make my peace with the situation. If I do not have a tumor, I will be very, very happy.

I like to remember that my family members have never had any serious illnesses: cancer, diabetes, arthritis, tumors, heart trouble. None of these troubled my parents, so why should they trouble me now?

I wish, though, that Monday would come and go. But you can't hurry time; nor can you hold it back. It passes at its own tempo and in its own way. I find I get along better if I keep busy doing things. This is not the period for solitude. I have caught up on my letters the past few days, done the budget, gone swimming every day, gone shopping when I need something, and picked and given away zinnias by the basketful. When Jane was here we went out for lunch, went for eggs and honey, and went for drives. Apprehension disperses when you are occupied or going somewhere. It also diminishes when you talk it out. Jane is a wonderful listener, and we have talked the situation over thoroughly. I *think* I can accept whatever develops. I wonder. I just have to contain myself until Monday. It will probably be Tuesday before I hear, or maybe even Wednesday–nearly a week. Oh, hum!

I have to pass the next few days somehow and not think too much about dying. You don't necessarily die if you have a tumor on the brain. I need to replace fear with faith. Can I do this? I will try.

I had the brain scan yesterday.

I am waiting, and waiting, and waiting now to hear the report from the doctor. Will it be normal or will there be a problem there? Who knows. I have some errands to run, but I had better stay right here and listen for the phone. I cleaned out the refrigerator, answered a letter, paid some bills, watered the plants.

What now? No telling how long I must wait, but wait I must. If I strung together all the hours I have waited for the doctors in my life, they would make quite a segment of time!

Perhaps I will make some zucchini bread. Emily gave me two zucchini squashes yesterday. I haven't made any in a long time. Yes, that is just what I shall do. That will take me an hour or so, and surely by then I will hear. Or will I?

It was pleasant making the zucchini bread. I really enjoyed mixing up the various ingredients, and it kept my mind occupied. It is in the oven now, and the whole apartment smells heavenly. This is a familiar fragrance these days in the halls of our buildings. As you walk by the single-story apartments now and then, you come upon this same delicious scent. This is one of my favorite fragrances of August.

There are many other fragrances of the month that I like also. When I walk down to the vegetable garden these days I breathe in the delicious meadow scent of midsummer. Wild meadows surround the vegetable gardens, and now they are ablaze with goldenrod and Queen Anne's lace. Some of the latter is going to seed, and the pods are attractive and interesting. There are flocks of butterflies in this meadow that I enjoy watching. They have such a charming and indirect approach to getting from here to there.

Another wonderful midsummer scent is the smell of all outdoors after it has been hot and dry for several days and it begins to rain. The water on the foliage emits a delicious odor. And who doesn't love the smell of fresh-cut grass?

Now the phone rings, and it is Alva, the nurse from the medical department. My test has come out perfectly normal. What a joyous moment! I feel limp with relief! I feel as if I have been given a magnificent present! I don't need to work on accepting the fact that I might die any more. I can accept the happy gift of life instead. The pills the doctor gave me have helped greatly, and my head is much better. So all is well. And August ends on this very cheerful note.

12 ❋

September Is Confidence

Season of mists and mellow fruitfulness
Close bosom-friend of the maturing sun.
            —John Keats, "To Autumn"

Those lines by Keats are September to me. These mornings I often waken to a world of mist. Sometimes my valley is totally hidden. When the sun shines through and melts the mist, it is thoroughly today. I get up eager to see what the day will bring. Before breakfast I go out and look at and appreciate my terrace garden. I have to— there are no two ways about it. My little weeping birch has developed the most charming catkins at the tips of its drooping branches. They look so tender and vulnerable. Pale green and tan they are. I feel them and they are firm and vital. Here in each of these little tails is the essence of the life of the tree. The chrysanthemums are flourishing; each plant has countless buds still to open. Every day more unfold. My three prunings worked. They are flowering and are quite low. They won't need staking at all. The plants are twice as large as last year and have an awful lot of blooms. The marigolds and ageratum are burgeoning, too; also the dwarf zinnias. A heavy mist is caught in the grass and sparkles in the sun.

Along the September roadsides goldenrod sweeps in great stretches. Here and there stands an occasional clump of joe-pye weed and a drift of purple asters. Fascinating milkweed pods are forming on the plants. The corn stalks so lush and green last month are browning these days. Acres of tan stubble show where a harvest has been gathered. And in the markets when you shop there is the luscious odor of ripe Concord grapes! To me, the essence of all of autumn is the fragrance of a single bunch of completely ripe Concord grapes!

I just realized something about myself and Crosslands.

One of the great challenges of growing older is to be able to find people who warmly receive and want and need what you have to give. How nourishing and fulfilling it is if, as the years gather, we are able continually to find such people.

I have been thinking about this lately and about how, when I lived in Tryon, there were many people who wanted what I had to give. Perhaps this is because they were old friends, friends of ten years' standing. When I was with people there I never felt I had to talk or create an impression. I just felt perfectly happy, and the conversation flowed along by itself. Lately, I have just realized, it is getting to be the same way here. I am pleased to be aware of this happening when my friendships are but four years old. I believe it is a matter of time and rapport before you develop an even exchange.

As well as spending a portion of our time with people who need and want what we have to give, we want to be on the receiving end when another gives of his or her uniqueness. These even exchanges deepen friendships and bring balance and a comfortable easiness to the relationship. It is best when the exchange is equal, when each is not only willing to receive what the other has to give, but also eager and needful of what the other offers.

As the month of September advances, we notice that summer is getting a little frayed about the edges. We observe the frayed edges of the leaves on some trees and other advanced signs of autumn here and there, such as the tall, tan grass in fields and along roadsides, the red fringes of sumac that greet us as we drive about, the charming owls at night in the valley hoo-oo-ing back and forth, and the barred owl who calls "who-cooks-for-you, who-cooks-for-you-all." We are willing to let go of summer with a loving backward glance or two in anticipation of the glory of October and what lies ahead.

At this time of year, with a season passing, there is a promise in all outdoors: in next year's dogwood buds, already on the trees, in the bulbs we see everywhere in the stores, and in the catalogs that arrive. There is the promise that spring will come. More than this, as we see nature prepare to change seasons, we sense another promise in the very air we breathe, a promise that even in this temperamental and unsure world there is reason and pattern all about us and a core of life that is even more powerful than stashed-away armaments. This is a month of promises, heartening ones.

The message of September is to build self-confidence. During the summer we have loosed and let go and relaxed into summer's leisurely pace. We have accepted what has come and taken all incidents in stride. We have counted our blessings. Now this is the time to gather ourselves together and consider if we need to build more self-confidence. Most of us do. There is a universal need to feel good about ourselves. Do we? Do we believe in ourselves? We all have times when we do and times when we don't, when we become a bit shaky inside.

We've all made mistakes and will probably continue to do so from time to time. We need to realize that mistakes are purely steps in learning and growing, not something to let haunt us.

People tend to think they should be perfect and never err. Everybody makes mistakes. We will make as many mistakes as our present state of growth and awareness permits. As we grow and develop more, we will make less, or perhaps we will make them on a higher level! But we are not our errors. We are much more than this.

Self-confidence is not self-love in an egotistical sense. In fact, boasting and self-praise are indications of inadequate self-confidence. Confidence is self-assurance without arrogance, courage without conceit.

Self-confidence is a feeling, not a mental concept of our assets. Nevertheless, an inventory of what we have done that came out well, that pleased us, that we can respect, is one good way to build confidence. Deep within us we all have an urge to express goodness and love. When we express the opposite we don't like ourselves and have no peace of mind. Losing peace of mind undermines confidence.

Increasing your peace of mind is one step toward having a good feeling about yourself and increasing confidence. Shedding all feelings of guilt is another. You can't just decide you are going to have peace of mind and shed guilt and have both happen immediately. You have to work at it. We all have to evolve our own rules for this. It involves attitudes. What happens doesn't matter; it is how we take it that is important and that brings either peace of mind and confidence to us or the opposite.

In life there is no way of telling what fabulous event will occur on any given day!

In my wildest imaginings I never thought we'd have a balloon landing on the grass outside the swimming pool. But after supper tonight we did. It was a gay balloon made of bands of many colors. There is a resident over at Kendal who was ninety years old today. Her son gave her a birthday present of a balloon ride—her first. The balloon arrived in Kendal in a truck all folded up. Quite a crowd of residents gathered around to watch as the balloon expert unfolded it. He then pumped hot air into it, settled his passengers, and took off. It rose gracefully into the air and drifted over the hilltop between Kendal and Crosslands. It came down on a large open space of grass by our pool.

By this time our residents had been alerted, and a large number were on hand for the landing. Everyone was much excited, especially the woman who had the birthday. She'd never had a birthday like this before. And she loved the ride. Then the balloon was deflated and folded up and put in the truck again. That was the excitement of the evening. Everything calmed down after that. The conversation settled around who would like to take a balloon ride and who would not. I am very content with the earth, and I was on the side of those who would not. But plenty of others said they would love it. However, no more rides tonight, the master of the balloon said as he took off in his truck.

There are many wonderful things about Crosslands. One thing I especially appreciate, which is part of the atmosphere, is that no one here ever feels sorry for himself or herself. No matter what the physical problem or difficult family situation, there are always others in the same predicament or worse. Not that everyone here has physical or family problems; but there are plenty who do. This is bound to be true of a group of four hundred people where the average age is seventy-eight. There are also large numbers of people here who are very well and healthy. There is a hiking group that takes a three-mile walk three times a week. There is Scottish dancing every Thursday evening, and many attend. There are avid and energetic gardeners, skaters on our pond here in winter, badminton players, and swimmers.

It is pretty nice to be among people who may have physical problems, but who are seldom sorry for themselves. One woman here has been in a wheelchair for years and will be the rest of her life. Recently she took up painting and had her work on exhibition, where it was much admired. At a church group, when asked her favorite Bible verse, she said "My cup runneth over."

What a glorious September day! Sparkling sunshine, blue sky, clear air, and massed clouds around the horizon. It rained in the night, and drops of water cling everywhere to the bushes and flowers. Each drop holds a rainbow complete if you look at it from the right angle. It is a garden of rainbows I have this morning.

First thing I did after breakfast was to go down to the vegetable gardens. Everything there was flourishing. In my plots I had quantities of tomatoes. I gathered some red and yellow ones and filled the bottom of the basket. They were large and firm and beautiful. I do think vegetables are as beautiful as flowers. Healthy, ripe produce is truly handsome. I cut broccoli, too, and picked a bowl of my first ripe raspberries. As I inadvertently stepped on a few leaves of tomatoes, the scent rose around me.

Various other people were down in their gardens. We all exchanged garden lore for a few minutes. My tall zinnias were a riot of color. I filled my basket with the fully cut flowers. I have such a variety of colors. I think I like the tawny shades the best: the yellows, oranges, flames, and the variations of these. I have some cactus flowered ones that are very nice, too.

Back at the apartment I arranged the flowers, putting some in each room, including the bathroom. I love having flowers in the bathroom, and the kitchen, too. I have three vases of flowers in the living room. And still I had plenty for neighbors. I shared my tomatoes, too. I will take some tomatoes over to the Center tonight to share with those I eat with. I don't know who I will be dining with, as I have no plan. It will be a pleasant surprise. It is fun to go over sometimes with no plan and just see who you are put with. This is a good way to get acquainted with people you don't know very well.

After sharing my flowers and tomatoes this morning, I drove down to Woodward's farm to get some sweet corn. I asked a friend to join me, and what a lunch we had! Corn on the cob, my broccoli, sliced red and yellow tomatoes, and raspberries. This is the kind of morning I love. Harvesting produce is so satisfying, especially now that the days are cooler and the air is crisp.

September is a wonderful month. During the first part there is all of summer's productiveness, and at the same time hints of fall fill the air. There is the promise of cool days ahead and a change of seasons coming.

I have three special friends whom I meet with occasionally to talk to about things of a deep nature. This week we began discussing faith. Of course, you could discuss faith indefinitely and still hardly scratch the surface. Our discussion was rich and rewarding.

One of the ideas we came up with is that faith seems to have no beginning and no end. It is always here, there, and everywhere. We could not function for a single hour without faith. We need faith in everything—our fellow man, our friends, our country, ourselves, God. Without faith, we would be nothing and get nowhere. We have faith in many physical things—in our cars, in the food we eat. We have faith that fall will come and then winter and then spring. We have faith that a bulb planted will grow and flower, that a plant set out will flourish and bloom. Without thinking about it, we are having faith all day long every day.

The kind of faith that calls upon our inner resources is faith in the intangibles. Emerson said, "All I have seen teaches me to trust the creator for all I have not seen."

Perhaps faith is the memory of spiritual experience. If we have had various positive experiences of having faith, we are inclined with Emerson to trust God that more will come.

It has been said, "Fear knocked on the door. Faith answered, and no one was there."

A thought-provoking comment on faith by Ambrose Worrall, the late spiritual healer, is, "Faith is the lack of resistance to that which you hope to receive."

I've been picking raspberries. What a bountiful crop I have! They are dead ripe and fall off in my hand. They are huge and luscious, and every now and then I have to eat one or two or three sun-warmed and dead ripe. I am eating dinner with Sally tonight, and we'll come back here for a dessert of raspberries, powdered sugar, and cream.

We've had some chilly nights. Is that why these last berries are so sweet and delicious? There are so many lasts this month: last tomatoes, each one might be the last, for we might get a frost at any time. They seem to hold the beneficence of the sun in their flavor, these remaining tomatoes. The vines are full. Will a lot of them go on ripening? And will the raspberries?

I was sitting quietly in the living room this evening hooking my rug, which I just got out today. I was recalling a luncheon this noon when one member of the group gave another member some unasked-for advice. I wondered at the time, how affected are other people by what we suggest they do?

Not so much, I think. I really question this business of giving advice. It immediately causes the one advised to feel inferior, and it assumes that the advisor has all the answers. Who has all the answers anyhow, or even a few answers? We may discover directions but not always answers, because answers are mysterious things. What is an answer to me is not necessarily an answer to you, and vice versa. What is an answer this week or this month may not be an answer next week or month; more likely it is a temporary direction. Answers have a way of not staying answers for long. And we naturally draw away from one who appears to have all of them.

In the long run, I believe other people are more affected by what we *are* than what we suggest or advise.

All of us can remember back to what someone said that affected us years ago or weeks ago or yesterday; but wasn't it always said by someone with no intention to influence or change us? Wasn't it what that person said that revealed what he or she basically and inwardly was? Maybe this inadvertent remark or conversation caused us to change directions or do something in life differently. But it was probably not because we were advised to.

I woke to a beautiful sunny day on this, my birthday. I am seventy-nine. How aged that seems as I think of it! I don't feel all that old. There are some things that I can't do that I used to do; but there are plenty of things I can do, too, like gardening, walking, swimming, sewing, entertaining, having parties, and such. My days are pleasantly filled, but not too full. I never like to be pressed for time. I have kept the promise I made to myself when I came here: not to live in a rush. That was for the beginning and middle parts of life. Now I have plenty of free time in every day—time for dreaming, for ruminating, for following the urges of the spirit. When people tell me they are so busy all the time, I feel that they want to be, and more power to them. I am content as I view my life—my long, leisurely mornings and afternoons; my casual walks; my afternoon swims, which I take if the spirit moves me to.

A birthday is a very special day, and it is linked with a lot of other birthdays. I lay in bed thinking about other birthdays I have had. I spent a little time this morning picking dead heads off the marigolds, grooming my chrysanthemums. Jane and Helen took me to the Market Place for lunch, and we had their superb mushroom melts. I slept after lunch, had a delightful swim, and Jane took me out for dinner to Chadd's Ford Inn. This was a special occasion. All day I felt happy as I considered my life here with the people I know and those I am getting to know. I received a number of birthday cards, and in the evening the children called. It was great to hear their voices all across the country, Bob and Tim and Joan.

I went to bed early, happy and peaceful, and watching the stars outside my window.

My birthday ended on this lovely note.

From raspberry time to raspberry time, from red sumac leaves to red sumac leaves, from little owls in the forest to little owls in the forest, we have come full circle through the twelve months of this last year, twelve months of gardening and being.

There have been ups and downs, high points and low, and through them all and because of them this year has been a learning, growing experience. The months of this year have had their messages. These months pass slowly through my mind now as I think back—change, appreciation, giving, holding, not hurrying, awareness, living in the moment, listening, loosing and letting go, accepting, counting blessings, and increasing self-confidence.

But this is only one year; there are many other years ahead and other months that will have different messages, different things to tell us. This is only a beginning.

In the years ahead numerous different experiences will come to us all, and they will point up other aspects of gardening and being. In this year we have touched some of the depths involved in gardening. We have been a part of some heightened moments of being.

There will be many more significant moments to participate and experience in both gardening and being for those who are open and ready, those who look and listen and learn.